Working with Gangs and Young People

of related interest

Working with Anger and Young People
Nick Luxmoore
ISBN 1 84310 466 0

Listening to Young People in School, Youth Work and Counselling
Nick Luxmoore
ISBN 1 85302 909 2

Violence in Children and Adolescents
Edited by Ved Varma
ISBN 1 85302 344 2

Communicating with Children and Adolescents
Action for Change
Edited by Anne Bannister and Annie Huntington
ISBN 1 84310 025 8

Adolescence
Assessing and Promoting Resilience in Vulnerable Children 3
Brigid Daniel and Sally Wassell
ISBN 1 84310 019 3

Children Taken Seriously
In Theory, Policy and Practice
Edited by Jan Mason and Toby Fattore
Foreword by Mary John
ISBN 1 84310 250 1

Shattered Lives
Children Who Live with Courage and Dignity
Camila Batmanghelidjh
ISBN 1 84310 434 2

Understanding Street Drugs
A Handbook of Substance Misuse for Parents, Teachers and Other Professionals
Second Edition
David Emmett and Graeme Nice
ISBN 1 84310 351 6

Understanding Drug Issues
A Photocopiable Resource Workbook
Second Edition
David Emmett and Graeme Nice
ISBN 1 84310 350 8

Working with Gangs and Young People

A Toolkit for Resolving Group Conflict

Jes   *and Nia Imani Kuum**ba**

Jes
Lo

Paranoia exercise (p.124) is adapted from *Geese Theatre Handbook* (Baim, Brookes and Mountford 2002; reprinted 2006), with kind permission of the Geese Theatre Company and Waterside Press, www.watersidepress.co.uk

First published in 2006
by Jessica Kingsley Publishers
116 Pentonville Road
London N1 9JB, UK
and
400 Market Street, Suite 400
Philadelphia, PA 19106, USA

www.jkp.com

Library of Congress Cataloging in Publication Data
Feinstein, Jessie, 1970-
Working with gangs and young people : a toolkit for resolving group conflict / Jessie Feinstein and Nia Imani Kuumba.
p. cm.
Includes bibliographical references.
ISBN-13: 978-1-84310-447-6 (pbk. : alk. paper)
ISBN-10: 1-84310-447-4 (pbk. : alk. paper) 1. Gangs. 2. Conflict management--Problems, exercises, etc. 3. Gang members--Psychology. 4. Social work with youth. I. Kuumba, Nia Imani, 1965- II. Title.
HV6437.F445 2006
364.4'4--dc22
                    2006013014

British Library Cataloguing in Publication Data
A CIP catalogue record for this book is available from the British Library

ISBN-13: 978 1 84310 447 6
ISBN-10: 1 84310 447 4

Printed and bound in Great Britain by
Printwise (Haverhill) Ltd, Suffolk

Contents

Preface

This manual is intended for all adults working with young people involved in group and gang conflict. It is the culmination of three years' action research with 14- to 25-year-olds carried out by Leap, exploring innovative and engaging ways of working with antagonistic groups.

The work is rooted in the principle that conflict is an inevitable part of life. If left unresolved it can be damaging. Conversely, if conflict is worked with creatively, it can be an opportunity for growth and change.

Since 1987, Leap Confronting Conflict has been providing opportunities for young people and adults to explore creative approaches to conflict in their lives, finding causes and new solutions for themselves. Some of the negative effects of gang activity on young people, their families and their communities have led to an increase in training requests for Leap to work in situations where issues of group identity, ethnicity and gang membership are significant. A pilot seminar run by Leap in 1999 on street gang activity attracted 40 practitioners from around the UK. No innovative UK-based models were identified, and a lack of inspiration and resources was apparent. Ninety-five per cent of information referring to gang interventions collected by the National Youth Agency relates to projects and models developed in the USA and Europe. (The National Youth Agency is a UK body that supports those involved with the personal and social development of young people.)

This prompted Leap to establish a Gangs and Territorialism Action Research project in January 2001. The project aimed to assess and implement good practice in supporting youth gang members in making healthy transitions to adulthood. The Gangs and Territorialism workers took a three-pronged approach to the action research: they undertook a review of academic and non-academic literature relating to gangs; they spoke to practitioners and academics in the UK, USA and Europe who were experienced in working with young people in gangs; and they ran focus groups with young people who were affected by gang activity.

From this research Leap has developed innovative ways to harness the energy and companionship of the gang into sources of new leadership and learning. This work enables young people to make informed choices about their behaviour, and heightens their understanding of the consequences of their decisions.

The manual presents new and practical resources that can be used to explore the intricacies of gang membership and group identity. The exercises can be used as part of an intensive programme of work with young people involved in gangs, or as materials integrated into other group work programmes.

Acknowledgements

The authors would like to thank the following people: Carey Haslam and Jo Broadwood for their continued wisdom, experience, clarity and generosity. Helen Carmichael for having the inspired forward thinking when planning both phases of the Gangs and Territorialism project. All the staff at Leap Confronting Conflict for their support; in particular John Dillon for the illustrations, formatting, and remaining cheerful and trainers René Manradge, Nik Pitcher and Tony Weekes for their thoughtful contributions and overview. Raj Bhari for sharing his experience of forum theatre. Mr and Mrs Feinstein for their proofreading and love. Simon Hepburn for the long conversations and insight offered and Pauline Mcfarlane for supporting Nia as he ate, slept and lived the work.

We are also greatly indebted to all the youth work practitioners and young people who participated in the focus groups, pilot projects, partnership projects and Gangs! What Gangs? conference for sharing their trust, time, ideas and experiences, which made this manual what it is; in particular Rubel Ahmed and Vicki Burns.

We would also like to thank the Gangs Advisory Panel, in particular Ian Suatt for his continued presence and intelligent questioning, Eliza Grainger for her input into the research and Professor Dave Brotherton for overseeing and evaluating the work.

Much of the material in this manual has evolved from others' work. Particular inspiration was gained from the earlier Leap publications, *Through the Walls* and *Playing with Fire*, with some of the exercises adapted directly from the materials designed by Nic Fine and Fi Macbeth (Fine 1996; Fine and Macbeth 1995). Ideas were drawn from many other sources, especially from the work of Geese Theatre Company and Auguste Boal.

We are enormously grateful to The Diana, Princess of Wales Memorial Fund and the Big Lottery Fund for providing the resources for phases one and two of the Gangs and Territorialism Project.

Introduction

Everybody has an opinion about young people, gangs and territorialism. It is held by some that there is a current gang problem of epidemic proportions. Alternatively, gangs may be viewed as supportive networks and the violence that accompanies being part of this friendship group as nothing more than the 'rough and tumble' of growing up. The challenge of defining gangs, alongside the difficulty of collecting data about their behaviour, results in problems gauging whether it is actual incidents of gang violence, reporting of gang violence or fear of gang violence that is on the increase. We do know that gang membership and activity come in a variety of forms and will vary from area to area. For instance, within cities a multitude of gangs will exist and their characteristics will be dependent on the local context, e.g. housing policy, ethnic mix, local geography and history.

The word 'gang' usually conjures up images of fear, danger, guns, knives, fighting in the streets, drugs and organised crime. Almost none of the current language really describes the more complex relationships that groups of young people develop with and between each other. The research carried out by Leap acknowledges that many young people are choosing gang participation as a means of making the transition through adolescence to adulthood. Gang membership can offer an important source of support to young people. However, it can also result in dangerous behaviour, which puts the young people involved at risk of harm and/or offending behaviour. In turn, this can create a sense of division, distrust and danger in the communities in which they live. For a fuller description of the methodology and learning from Leap's research see the Appendix at the end of this book.

What is a gang?

There are many different types of gang and also many different types of groups that might be labelled as gangs. In the UK, gangs are often loose associations of friends and only a minority of groups are 'US-style', organised, hierarchical, criminally active armed young people. The one common denominator is that all groups, whether defining themselves as gangs or friendship groups, get into violent confrontations with other gangs and groups. The factors fuelling these conflicts vary enormously: for example, arguments over girlfriends or boyfriends, disputes over drugs, the 'disrespect' of one gang entering another's territory.

Why are young people in gangs?

Group membership is a natural part of the transition to adulthood for most young people. For many gang members the gang is a source of friendship and enjoyment. It offers protection to its members and also provides them with something to do. Many young people in gangs have poor school achievement records and limited access to training and employment, which often results in low self-esteem. Being in a gang can provide a way of attaining a sense of belonging, power, status and safety when it is not being found in other areas of young people's lives. The violence accompanying gang membership gives the young people a sense of excitement and an adrenalin buzz as well as strengthening their group identity.

What is the difference between a gang and a group of friends?

Self-proclaimed gang and non-gang members tend to differ most significantly in terms of self-classification rather than criminal conduct. The most noteworthy difference between gang and non-gang members' criminal conduct relates to the kind of antisocial conduct they carry out. Gang members are more likely to engage in criminal conduct that is visible and in the company of others, e.g. graffiti or group fighting. This may reflect their desire to communicate a particular impression or reputation to fellow members and wider society. Young people tend to be considered to be a gang by other people in the community when they are seen as threatening and deeply rooted in an area. Often a group of young people will not consider themselves to be in a gang, yet when describing their rivals (who usually share many attributes) they will consider this group to be a gang.

There are many costs and many gains to gang membership. The exercises in this manual are not designed to cause young people to leave the gang, but to make informed decisions about their gang membership. By exploring the benefits and disadvantages of gang membership, young people will be in a better position to make choices that will keep them safe and support them in getting where they want to be in society. The materials in this manual have been thoroughly tested and revised to ensure their relevance and applicability.

How to Use this Manual

Who is this manual for?

This manual is designed for adults who work with young people involved in gang and group conflict. Ideally those using this manual will have some experience of facilitating groupwork, although this is not a necessity. The work has been developed to explore the dynamics, bonds and conflicts that exist within friendship groups and gangs. For that reason, the exercises are most effective when used with a group that has a long history together rather than a group that has come together due to circumstance, such as a school tutor group.

If you are working with a group of young people who are involved in or affected by gangs but do not form a gang, this material can be adapted. For example, if this material is being used with a group of young people in prison, more emphasis may be placed on exercises that explore individual relationships towards the gang as opposed to the group's dynamics.

Setting the agenda

The manual is set out in four chapters. Each chapter explores a different theme through a variety of exercises that constitute a full day workshop. The material has been designed so that it can be tailored to suit the needs of the groups and their facilitators. For example, if the groups are coming in for six 2-hour sessions the facilitator can choose a selection of exercises that are of most relevance. In doing this it is suggested that a format similar to that of the full day workshops is used, i.e. starting with a gathering and a game (see below for description) and having a break mid-way. If exercises are chosen randomly from this manual it will be important for facilitators to find and explore the links between the exercises.

It is a good idea in the very first session to follow the day plan for Safety and Danger as these exercises are vital both in introducing the issue of gangs and establishing safety in the training room (see Exercises 1.2 to 1.4, pp.27–32).

Setting up the room

The training room used should have as few distractions as possible, and certainly no interruptions. Many of the exercises involve moving around so consideration must be given to the size of the space. Chairs need to be set out in a circle prior to participants entering the room. Flip-chart pens and paper ought to be available in the room and any notes taken should be put up on the wall. After each session they should be taken down if someone else is using the room, kept safely, and then put back up before the start of the next session. This allows participants to see and refer to the work they have already done.

Facilitation style

We would recommend that this work take place with two facilitators in the room. This allows the facilitators to support one another as well as role model good teamwork. Having more than one facilitator helps to balance the energy, strengths and different styles of facilitation. It also means that when the group is split in two each group has its own facilitator. Wherever possible the facilitators should reflect a mix of ethnicity and gender.

At times participants will be revealing some intimate details about their lives and it is important that they feel safe in the process. The facilitators sharing some personal details from their own lives can encourage young people to do the same. The facilitator should think in advance about what they are willing to share with a group.

A sense of safety can also be promoted through a clearly defined structure. It is useful to have a session plan showing the timescale of the exercises and the breaks shared, approved and visible to participants. Timing the session effectively will promote discipline in the group and keep the pace fresh and exciting. All instructions need to be given clearly and the facilitator should give the participants opportunities to check understanding.

Ideally the group size would be between 8 and 14 people. Any more than 16 would require a third facilitator.

Explaining the techniques

The key to effective gangs groupwork is in the exploration of the exercises. Often the heart of the learning takes place in the 'Exploration' – the questioning sets at the end of each exercise. The philosophy behind this style of facilitation is that participants will learn by doing and reflecting on their own experiences, rather than being told. This is known as experiential learning. A wide variety of training techniques is evident in this manual to account for the different learning styles of participants.

Introducing the session

At the beginning of each session it is helpful to be clear about the aims and objectives of the training. Having these written up in advance can support young people's understanding. If it is the first time working with a group it can be useful to share with them the different ways of working, for example, games, small groupwork, large groupwork, drama, etc. Consideration can also be given to how the facilitators want to introduce themselves, such as a brief story about why they do the work they do or an experience of group conflict. The beginning of the session is also an opportunity for housekeeping, where information is given about issues such as smoking, fire drills and toilets.

Gatherings

A gathering is a groupwork tool used to focus a group on either a particular topic or simply on the fact that the group is beginning or ending a session. In a gathering, each participant takes it in turn to reflect on a topic. The depth of the topic can vary, e.g. 'Tell us about a place you feel safe', 'Tell us something you are looking forward to doing tonight'.

Gatherings literally gather the participants' thoughts on a particular topic. Suggested topics have been put into the programme plans in this manual. However, the facilitators can incorporate their own topics as they please. One of the facilitators introduces the topic and gives an example. They then choose whether to send the gathering to the left or the right. Whenever possible they should choose the direction so that the participants who are most likely to struggle are not first. If a participant cannot think of anything to say they can pass and they will be returned to once everyone else has spoken. Participants may need to be encouraged to think of different things rather than saying 'the same'. If a participant is struggling or straying off the focus they can be given support by the facilitator.

Games

There are many reasons for incorporating games into the groupwork. The right game at the right time can pick up the energy level in the room or provide light relief from more intense work. Some of the games develop particular themes such as trust, while others are there just for fun. All of the games in this manual include debriefing questions. These help to develop learning from the games around the themes of the workshop. Facilitators may choose not to debrief the games and simply let them stand alone.

Wordstorms

This is a technique for gathering information about a particular issue. The facilitator asks the group a question, e.g. 'What does the word 'enemy' mean to you?', and then writes all their responses on a piece of flip-chart paper. If a comment is not relevant or is said as a joke, the facilitator can ask the participant to say a little more about the suggestion until there is some clarity.

Input

This is simply where the facilitator gives the group information.

Exploration

After most of the exercises there are sets of exploration questions. The facilitator need not ask all the debriefing questions, just the ones they find appropriate.

Comments

After most exercises there are some comments about possible conversations that might arise from the exercise. These comments are based on experiences of running the exercises with different groups. The exercises are set out so that there is a natural progression from one exercise to the next. Thinking about the links between the exercises adds fluidity and meaning to the programme.

Tableau

Tableau is a technique used throughout this manual. In a tableau exercise individuals, pairs or groups of participants are asked to shape their bodies (or somebody else's) around a particular theme. For example, if the theme was success they might stand tall with their fists clenched above their head, as if on the winner's rostrum. A tableau is like a frozen image or a snapshot. It is a very useful technique as it often allows participants to be extremely expressive without having to find words.

Before asking participants to create a tableau, the facilitator should demonstrate the technique so that the participants are clear what is being asked of them. The facilitator manages the tableau by giving the participants a space to show back their image. This may mean creating a 'stage' so that all the chairs are lined up facing the same way. The facilitator counts down from three and then asks the participant(s) to hold the image. The 'audience' is then invited to get up and look around the image if they want to. Unless they are invited to, they should not touch the image. Once the image has been shown the facilitator can use a variety of techniques to process the tableau. Processing is a way of developing the learning through questioning and discussion.

There are many ways to process a tableau. One of the simplest ways is to ask each person to express a thought and feeling relating to their character's pose. The character can also be asked to show the action directly after the pose. Processing allows the facilitator to delve further into the character's experience without having to probe into the participant's real life experience. Although the experiences may be similar, tableau offers an opportunity to remove the participant from the experience, which may make it easier for them to use descriptive language. It can also highlight a different perspective on an event: e.g. the participant may be asked to express the thoughts and feelings of the mother of someone seriously hurt in a gang fight. Tableau is a particularly useful tool for participants to tell their story, especially when working with young men who struggle to describe their feelings or where English is a second language. It can create a powerful shared experience as participants may recognise themselves in others' images.

Processing can also involve the audience in the work. When the tableau is shown back, the audience may be asked to guess what is going on in the scene. Alternatively, once the scene has been developed, a volunteer from the audience can take the place of someone in the tableau. This allows the participant involved in the tableau to step outside the scene and observe another participant's take on the situation.

Role-play

Role-play is different from tableau in that it is more like acting as the role-player moves and speaks. Role-play is used in many different ways throughout this manual. It can be used both to enact real life scenarios with the role-players playing themselves or alternatively participants can take on characters very different from themselves. When role-playing real life scenarios, participants have the opportunity to explore different situations, e.g. a difficult conversation they are planning to have with someone. When participants take on imaginary characters the process becomes one step removed from reality, thus giving the role-players an opportunity to see a situation from other people's perspectives. It is useful to give the imaginary character a nametag so they are not called by their real name, thus blurring boundaries.

In the set-up of the role-play it is helpful to be clear about guidelines, e.g. agreement reached around use of swearing and physical touch. It is also useful in the set-up to be clear about the aims and focus of the role-play, individual tasks and practicalities such as numbers and timing.

De-roling

De-roling is a simple process that should take place after participants have been in character in a tableau or role-playing exercise. The aim is for participants to leave behind the character and return to being themselves. The facilitator may first ask the participant if there is anything they want to say in character before leaving the role. If they have a nametag they take it off and they may also be asked to do something physical, e.g. change chairs or turn around. The participant is then asked if there is anything they want to say to their character. They can also be asked to think of one similarity and one difference between themselves and their character. Finally, the participant will be asked a series of questions relating to themselves, e.g. 'What is your name?' 'What did you have for breakfast?' 'What is your favourite colour?'

Forum theatre

This is a process in which participants have the opportunity to create a role-play with which the audience interacts. When using forum theatre the group is split into two. The groups are given a scenario to devise a story around. Exercises such as Choices And Consequences (p.51) can be a good starting point for this. To encourage participants to think about their characters the technique of 'hot seating' can be used. This is a process whereby the participant is asked a series of questions in character, e.g. 'What's your name?' 'How many brothers do you have?' 'Do you smoke?' 'What are you usually doing at 9p.m. on a Saturday?'

The two groups then show their role-plays to each other. The first group performs their play the whole way through. They then show it again. However, this time the audience has the opportunity to stop the action and make suggestions to the character about how they could do things differently; e.g. a young man has been stopped by the police and swears at the police officer. The suggestion may be that the young man is polite to the police officer. The facilitator controls the process of the audience, halting the action by playing the role of the joker. The joker fields comments from the audience. If the suggestion from the audience is realistic the character will try out the suggestion. If they struggle with the suggestion a member of the audience can be asked to temporarily step into the action and try out the suggestion. The role-play continues in this manner until it has been shown back twice. This technique was pioneered by Auguste Boal and is described in detail in his book *Games for Actors and Non-Actors* (1992).

Safety

Context

When working with gangs it is usually relevant to work with the realities of the conflict the group is involved with. For example, if Gang A and Gang B have been fighting for five years the groupwork should explore the specific incidents that have taken place. Facilitators must be very clear that they are bound by law to report any information they have relating to a crime that has been committed or any crime that is due to be committed. Maintaining confidentiality is very important in order to provide a safe environment and the issue needs to be explored fully with young people to ensure they understand the limits of confidentiality. This may mean that in some instances it is more fruitful to work around an imaginary scenario than a real one.

Ground rules

An underlying philosophy of this work is the creation of relationship with a group and then the creation of boundaries within this relationship. Before embarking on a groupwork programme it is necessary to set up ground rules. This is a set of rules that encourages participation, allows for appropriate challenge and promotes safety. The group should jointly negotiate and agree the contract so that they 'own' the rules. If a participant is struggling with any part of the contract they should be offered some coaching around this. Coaching is a conversation that supports the participant in sticking to the ground rules. It can take place either in the training room or in a private space. Participants need to give their permission to the facilitator to be coached. As part of coaching the participant will be asked to make a commitment to change their behaviour.

As part of the contract, sanctions should be agreed if the contract is broken. This will involve setting clear parameters around what behaviour would result in a participant being asked to leave, how long they should be excluded for, and if and how they might re-enter the group.

Our experience of working with gangs shows the importance of having the gang's leader on board. Careful preparatory work needs to take place with this person, as without their support the groupwork has the potential to be unsuccessful.

Working with challenging behaviour

There are numerous types of challenging behaviour to be expected. These instances can be viewed as an opportunity for learning and transformation. As this work is of a self-exploratory nature, one of the key principles of this work is for the facilitator to be willing to look at their personal relationship with conflict. The facilitator's ways of dealing with conflict are often tested in moments of challenge from young people. Different facilitators will find different behaviour challenging. For example, one facilitator may struggle if a participant makes homophobic jokes; another may take exception to being sworn at. What the facilitator does in those moments of challenge is important in terms of creating and maintaining the relationship with the group and the learning in the training room. How well they cope with challenging behaviour will depend on their own levels of self-awareness, their experience of working with young people and their commitment to developing their own skills in conflict situations. If facilitators are aware of the areas they find challenging it is a good idea to discuss this with their co-facilitator so that they can offer support when the situation arises. Prior to facilitating 'confronting conflict' work it is useful for facilitators to undertake some specific training exploring their own approaches to conflict and facilitation of challenging behaviour from young people.

Captive vs. voluntary

The gang's response to the groupwork will vary depending on whether they have chosen to attend sessions or if they are duty bound to be there. If they are there voluntarily they are more likely to give permission to the facilitator to work with them.

In some instances it may feel appropriate to offer participants incentives to attend the sessions. Refreshments often entice young people although it is a good idea to manage the balance between what the group wants and avoiding foods overloaded with sugar that give them an energy buzz then drop. Group activities are a great way for the gang to enjoy positive activities as a friendship group. These activities can also act as a fascinating medium to explore the dynamics of the group once back in the training room. Vouchers can also be awarded to encourage young people to attend sessions. Finally, a residential trip often gives a group an incentive as well as providing them with an opportunity to do some more intense groupwork.

If your group is not there voluntarily, i.e. as part of a Supervision Order plan, the facilitator will have to pay extra attention to 'enrolling' the young people in the programme. Enrolling could involve having individual meetings with the young people prior to the start of the programme. This may also involve exploring the particular and specific benefits each young person may get from participating and individual goal setting. The aim is for participants to enrol in the programme so that they are in it for themselves rather than being there out of duty.

Measuring the effectiveness of the groupwork

Each individual programme will have a unique set of intended learning outcomes. Soft outcomes are more difficult to evaluate because they involve the measurement of outcomes such as increased self-esteem or increased sense of safety in the community. Hard outcomes are more straightforward to measure as they are more tangible, e.g. the number of young people entering training or employment as a direct consequence of the programme. Both soft and hard outcomes can be measured effectively by using a carefully designed evaluation tool. This tool can be used at the beginning of the programme to gauge where participants are (baseline assessment) and at the end of the programme to measure distance travelled.

Bringing rival gangs together

Often when groups that are in conflict are asked what they would like to gain from gangs work they state that they would like the opportunity to meet their rival gang. On the surface this may seem like a straightforward and sensible approach to addressing the conflicts between the groups. In reality, bringing rival groups together is an extremely challenging and delicate process, and it may not always be appropriate for rival groups to meet.

The many benefits of gang membership include a sense of excitement, safety, status, power, self-esteem and belonging – all feelings that are important for young people to experience. If gang conflict is entrenched there is a possibility that a peaceful reconciliation will result in confusion and a loss of status for influential gang members once the 'enemy' is removed. As a result gang members may deliberately or unconsciously sabotage any reconciliation process.

When gang members have known little other than group conflict and having a common enemy, a resolution to that conflict can leave a void in young people's lives. For instance, one of the by-products of the peace process in Northern Ireland was that some people who had been embroiled in the conflict for many years, and had known little else than living to fight the enemy, were left in organised groups without a political cause to fight. This led to some of the paramilitary groups becoming organised criminal gangs as well as gang fighting within the Protestant and Catholic communities. In instances of entrenched conflict, careful work needs to be done with individuals in the gang to explore the development of alternative sources of status, power and self-esteem.

For some of the young people in gangs that have low self-esteem and uncertainty about their role and status in society, the process of participating in a gangs programme will be a struggle. If they are only just beginning to explore their own feelings around their identity and status it may be too high an expectation that they also work towards reconciliation with their 'enemy' directly. However, it can still be fruitful to have the participants focus on their enemies in groupwork sessions. For instance, effective work can take place by asking the groups to build a tableau of how they think the other gang may feel about specific incidents, e.g. the injury or incarceration of one of their members. It is a beginning for the gangs to be thinking about their rivals' thoughts and feelings and a step towards a meeting in the future.

When groups have participated in a programme and it feels productive to bring the gangs together, the process will need to be managed very carefully, with attention paid to specific individuals within the groups. Successful joint sessions hinge on gently balancing the need for justice to be restored with the need for pride to remain intact. For instance, one of the groups may feel they 'deserve' to get revenge and agreement will need to be reached regarding what could happen that would keep them happy without antagonising their rivals.

If it has been agreed that it would be fruitful for rival gangs to meet, a good deal of planning will need to take place around preparing the groups and the content of the sessions. For further discussion around possible content and outcomes of joint meetings see Taking the Work Forward (p.129). Joint sessions should take place in a neutral space that has enough private rooms for each gang present. Workers attached to each group need to be involved at every stage and the gangs themselves will need to have done some intensive work as a group beforehand.

Before bringing the groups together for a joint session each group should be prepared in pre-meetings. In these meetings the purpose of the joint meeting is explored and the following questions are useful:

- Why do you think you're meeting?

- What do you think is going to happen?

- What would you like the outcome to be?

- What do you think would help the process?

- What might get in the way?

- Are you worried about anything in particular?

- What if someone says something you don't like?

- What will you do?

- What shall we do if it's not working?

- What might block you?

- Who in your group is most likely to lose their temper?

- How can you support them?

- Is there anybody in the other group you have particular concerns about?

- Do you want the police to be informed of the meeting?

- Do you want a weapons check to take place?

In some circumstances it may feel appropriate for the group to select representatives to attend a smaller meeting. In these instances the gangs should be encouraged to think carefully about the skills each other possesses that will help the meeting to be productive, e.g. communication skills, ability to control temper, diplomacy. We have worked with one group that hoped to send their best communicator and their best fighter, based on the logic that if communication broke down they would be in a strong position physically. This group was encouraged to change their mindset about the meeting in the hope that a more optimistic perspective would impact on the meeting.

When only representatives of each group are meeting, careful attention should be paid to reintegration into their group. For instance, a meeting was established in Belfast, Northern Ireland, to explore different perspectives on the Marching Season. (The Marching Season is a series of marches in which the Loyalist community commemorate the Battle of the Boyne. In recent years these marches have caused conflict because the Protestant Loyalists hoped to march through traditionally Catholic areas.) Some of the representatives encountered hostility and suspicion when they returned to their own communities simply for being in the same room as their 'enemies'. Work should take place with these groups exploring the impact of representatives returning to their group before anybody meets. Once joint meetings have taken place, care should be taken in the follow-up. If just one joint meeting is planned it is useful to arrange a review meeting with each group to explore any developments since the meeting.

Chapter 1

Safety and Danger

> I would always look to help my mates; once I nearly died due to my mates… I was in hospital and all that. On a few occasions my friend called me and said to me he was in trouble with a gang and they were going to cut him up… I went over there just to make sure he was OK.
>
> *Participant from Leap's action research project*

The gang offers a wild kind of safe space where young people can experience alternative parenting, support and protection. In order to grow and thrive it is important to feel protected. Often young people do not feel protected by the police or their families. To feel safe they must be able to protect themselves against whatever threatens them.

When we asked young people why they were in gangs they told us that the excitement and protection the gang offered was most important for them. The excitement is often the high of danger that comes with lawbreaking and fighting. The protection relates to 'safety in numbers' and 'having each other's backs'. Ultimately, safety and danger are two sides of the same coin. However, which side the coin falls is often beyond the gang member's control.

The essence of this work is to explore with young people what choices they have when the coin falls and what are the possible consequences of these choices. The hope is that when faced with challenging situations they will make informed choices that will be most likely to take them to where they want to be.

The unspoken honour code of gangs dictates that gang members do not snitch on each other and they back each other up no matter what. The bond and sense of belonging created by this loyalty provides a safety net for young people who may feel marginalised from a hostile society.

Key questions

It is the dynamics of this safe space that we seek to explore in this chapter. Thorough examination of the intricacies of gang membership and group identity will prompt young people to ask:

- Who am I?

- Who am I in relation to the gang?

- How can I be safe?

- Is there safety in numbers?

- Who can I trust?

- What choices do I have?

Aims

- To explore the advantages and disadvantages of being in a gang.

- To look at the unwritten rules of gang membership.

- To focus on the costs and gains of providing back up to friends.

- To understand who protects you and who you protect.

- To develop more choices when confronted with potentially violent situations.

Safety and Danger Day Plan

Day Intro – Day outline, programme outline, ways of working, facilitators' intros	10.00	10 min
Gathering – Name and what you hope to get from the day	10.10	10 min
Game – Sun Shines On	10.20	15 min
What Is A Gang?	10.35	20 min
Unwritten Rules	10.55	15 min
BREAK	11.10	20 min
Ground Rules	11.30	30 min
Where Do You Stand?	12.00	20 min
Red Flags	12.20	40 min
LUNCH	1.00	60 min
Gathering – A place you feel safe	2.00	10 min
Game – Sharks	2.10	10 min
FIDO	2.20	40 min
24/7 Conflict Street	3.00	30 min
BREAK	3.30	20 min
Game – Blame Game	3.50	15 min
Choices And Consequences	4.05	45 min
Close – Something you have learned today	4.50	10 min

1.1 Sun Shines On

Time: 15 min

Explanation

An active whole group game.

Intention

To begin thinking about different types of conflict.

Instructions

1. The facilitator asks the participants to sit in a circle and removes any empty chairs, including their own.

2. The facilitator explains that the aim of the game is for participants to find a seat and that the way they will do this is to make a statement that is visible and true about themself, e.g. 'The sun shines on everybody with brown eyes.' At this point everybody who has brown eyes will stand up and switch seats.

3. The facilitator then introduces two further rules. Participants cannot go back to the seat they got up from and they may not switch to the seat directly next to them on either side.

4. Once participants have got the hang of the game the facilitator moves it on to visible things they might have in common, e.g. family, hobbies.

5. The final stage of the game is for the subject to change once more to anything to do with conflict, e.g. 'The sun shines on everybody who has ever argued with a brother or a sister.' The subject can then be changed to group conflict, e.g. 'The sun shines on everybody who has been in a fight with more than three people.'

6. The facilitator judges an appropriate time for the game to end.

Exploration

- What was it like to play the game?

- How did you feel standing in the middle?

- How did you feel when you were looking for a seat?

- What was it like if only a few people moved?

- What was it like when everyone moved?

Comments

This exercise is a gentle introduction to looking at the vast array of conflicts we experience in life. Participants may learn things they didn't know about each other and it is an opportunity for the facilitators to share personal information with the group. To avoid participants directing offensive comments at each other it is very important to strictly enforce the rule of it having to be true about yourself. This exercise can also be used to begin to explore some of the themes of safety and danger. The debriefing questions could lead to a conversation about different types of safety. As well as physical safety it is important to feel safe internally. For some participants it will be difficult to be in the centre of the circle and they may experience a lack of safety.

1.2 What Is A Gang?

Time: 20 min

Explanation

A whole group wordstorming exercise and discussion exploring gang membership.

Intention

To explore differences between gang and group membership.

Instructions

1. The facilitator writes the phrase 'What is a gang?' in the middle of a piece of flip-chart paper and invites the participants to call out the first thoughts that come into their heads in response to this question. The following prompts can be used:

    *   Think about gangs in your particular area.

    *   What comes to mind when you hear about gangs of youths rioting?

2. Next the facilitator takes a fresh piece of flip-chart paper and goes through the same process with the question 'Why are young people in gangs?'

3. The facilitator asks the participants to have a look at the second piece of paper and identify which words on the sheet are true for them. The facilitator then puts a circle around those words, explaining that they will circle the word even if it is only true for one person. For example, one participant may say they spend time with their friends because it gives them status, so status would be circled regardless of whether or not it is true for anyone else in the group.

Exploration

*   What were some of the differences/similarities between your group of friends and a gang?

*   What are the gains of being in a gang?

*   What are the costs of being in a gang?

*   When people see you and your friends on the street do you think they see you as a group of friends or a gang?

*   Do you consider yourself to be in a gang?

*   Who decides whether or not you're in a gang?

Comments

This exercise begins unpicking the question at the heart of gangs work: what does being in a gang give to/take away from your life? We have run this exercise over 40 times and despite a multitude of responses the words group, fun, protection and belonging are nearly always written up. It may be interesting to point out to the group that these words have either neutral or positive connotations and then lead into a discussion exploring what is it about gangs that is negative or causes difficulties for its members.

1.3 Unwritten Rules

Time: 15 min

Explanation

A whole group exercise in which participants are asked individually to identify their unwritten rules.

Intention

To look at why we have unwritten rules and where they come from.

Instructions

1. The facilitator begins by asking the participants why there are rules in society. They then ask if having rules is a good thing. The facilitator can give an example of what society might be like without rules, e.g. 'I could go into your house and steal your stereo.'

2. The facilitator then asks the group to distinguish between laws, e.g. stealing, and unwritten rules, e.g. pushing in front of someone in a queue.

3. Next the facilitator asks if there are any unwritten rules relating to their gang/group, e.g. backing each other up. The facilitator then inputs that everybody has unwritten rules. These are things which are important to us that other people might not be aware of.

4. The facilitator gives an example of two unwritten rules they have, e.g. no one touches my hair, people shouldn't leave washing up in the sink.

5. The participants are then asked to get into pairs and discuss two unwritten rules that they have. The first is a personal unwritten rule and the second is one that relates to the gang/group.

6. Each pair then feeds their unwritten rules back to the group.

Exploration

- How do you let people know your personal unwritten rules?

- What happens if these are broken?

- How does it feel when an unwritten rule is broken?

- How do you let people know your group/gang's unwritten rules?

- What happens if these are broken?

- What can happen if other people know your unwritten rules?

- Where do unwritten rules come from?

- Why do we have these rules?

- How do they support us?

- Who enforces the gang's unwritten rules?

- How are they enforced?

Comments

Although the groups we have worked with are very clear about the gang's unwritten rules this may be the first time they are spoken about in these terms. Sometimes the group may discover variations in the group's unwritten rules and this may provoke a difficult conversation among them. For example, an individual in the group may be criticised for behaviour which goes against a group unwritten rule, such as running away from a fight. It is important that the facilitator encourages the group to discuss the differences in perception in a way that is safe for all and does not demonise or exclude any individual. The facilitator might use a specific exercise to explore the issues further, e.g. Where Do You Stand? (p.33).

1.4 Ground Rules

Time: 30 min

Explanation

A small group exercise in which participants are asked to devise a contract for the group that defines acceptable and unacceptable behaviour.

Intention

To create safety in the room and to help facilitation.

Instructions

1. The facilitator asks the participants a series of questions about contracts: e.g. 'What is a contract?' 'What sorts of people have contracts?' 'Does anyone in the room have a contract?' 'Why do we have contracts?' 'What sorts of contract are there?'

2. The facilitator then explains that the participants are going to create a behaviour contract to make the groupwork environment safe for all participants. The facilitator asks the participants to give examples of ground rules they would like to see which would help them to participate in the session and create safety, e.g. allow each other space to speak.

3. The participants are then split into smaller groups of approximately four. Each group must come up with four ground rules.

4. Once all the groups have finished the large group is brought back together to share their ideas.

5. The ground rules are then written up clearly on a piece of flip-chart paper. If some groups give the same ground rules they do not need to be written twice.

6. As the ground rules are being written up the facilitator checks everyone's understanding or asks for clarification on anything that isn't clear, e.g. what exactly does 'respect' mean?

7. The facilitator then asks the group to agree what should happen if someone breaks the ground rules. At this point it is important for the participants to agree on sanctions. It is a good idea for the facilitator to have a clear idea of how they will support participants to stick to the contract. It is also useful if they have thought about any ground rules they would like as well as having input on the sanctions. (For further discussion see the section on safety, p.17.)

Comments

The centre in which the group is meeting may have its own ground rules and it is worth checking what these are and what may need to be added to them. Wherever possible it is helpful if the rules are couched in positive language, for example, 'allow each other the space to speak', as opposed to more negative language such as 'no interrupting'. The question of mobile phones is often contentious and you may need to negotiate that phones can be left on silent and that any urgent calls must be taken outside the room.

1.5 Where Do You Stand?

Time: 20 min

Explanation

A group exercise in which participants are invited to explore a range of themes related to safety and danger.

Intention

To explore thinking about safety and danger and locate areas of difference and consensus within the group.

Instructions

1. The facilitator marks one end of the room as 'agree' and the other as 'disagree' and the middle of the room as 'maybe' or 'not sure'. The participants are told they will be read a series of statements and that they should place themselves in the room depending on their thoughts about this statement. They can stand anywhere along the continuum line. Participants can move position if something is said that gives them a new perspective on the statement.

2. The facilitator reads out the statements:

    - You should back up your friends no matter what.

    - I feel safer in my area than outside it.

    - If you dress a certain way you can avoid trouble.

    - I feel safe when I'm with my friends.

3. After each statement is read out the participants move into position. The facilitator chooses members of the group representing different opinions to explain their positions. The facilitator can explore any of the participant's positions.

Exploration

- How does being in a gang create safety?

- How does being in the gang create danger?

- What do you do to keep safe?

- What was it like to share your point of view/be listened to?

- What usually happens when someone has a different point of view from you?

- Was it difficult to take up a different position from your friends?

- How did it feel if you changed position?

- What made you change position?

- Did it feel better to be in the outside positions or the middle positions?

- If everyone agrees, does it make it right?

Comments

The key to this exercise is the exploration of the participant's point of view. In the first question we have had some interesting discussion and shifts in position after exploration of the *no matter what* part of the question, e.g. 'If your friend robbed an old lady/sexually assaulted someone would you still back them up?' The facilitator can choose to be as provocative as they deem appropriate and substitute questions depending on the local context and relevant to the issues that they are already picking up from working with the group.

1.6 Red Flags

Time: 40 min

Explanation

A short role-play exercise exploring our emotional reactions in conflict situations.

Intention

To look at what triggers our emotional reactions to conflict situations and what happens to us when they are triggered.

Instructions

1. The facilitator asks the participants questions relating to a Spanish bullfight, e.g. 'Have you ever seen a Spanish bullfight?' 'What happens?' 'Why does the bull charge and act in an aggressive manner?'

2. The facilitator inputs that the bull charges at the flag because waving the material triggers the bull into a reaction. Similarly, in life there are situations that provoke a strong reaction in us. It is our normal reaction to a situation and it is automatic. We call this a red flag, as it is a situation in which we react when someone says or does something to us.

3. The facilitator gives an example of one of their red flags: e.g. If I leave my belongings on a chair and somebody moves them to the floor or if I am accused of stealing something.

4. The facilitator asks the participants if they can think of any examples of a red flag for themselves.

5. The facilitator then demonstrates a 30-second role-play of one of their red flags. Before showing the role-play they tell the participants where it is happening and who else is there. The facilitator shows the role-play, stopping just at the point where they are about to go into reaction. After showing the action the facilitator asks the following five questions:

    - What is the red flag?
      Somebody moving my belongings without asking.

    - What do you think when this happens?
      They are disrespecting me.

    - How do you feel when this happens?
      I feel violated.

    - Where do you feel it in your body?
      My chest tightens.

- What would you like to be different?

   I would like them to ask if they can move my belongings.

6. The facilitator then asks participants to choose a situation in which another person says or does something that upsets or angers them. The participants work in pairs and rehearse the short role-plays. They should choose a situation each so that they have two short scenes to show back to the rest of the group.

7. Participants show back their role plays (as in instructions in item 5). The responses to the questions should be noted on a flip chart. If several of the participants feel 'angry' when the red flag is waved, the facilitator can ask them to rate their level of anger from 1 to 10.

Exploration

- Do any of the scenes have anything in common?

- Is it important to know your own red flags?

- What can you do if you know your own red flags?

- How many red flags do you have?

- Do you think that you know all your red flags?

- Do you know each other's red flags?

- Has anyone known what someone's red flag is and used it to wind them up?

- As a group, do you have a red flag?

- Do you know a red flag for the group you're in conflict with?

- When your red flag is waved, who has the power?

- Where in your body do you feel anger?

- What are the physical signs that you are getting angry?

- What did you notice about where and how others feel feelings?

Comments

It is interesting that the majority of responses to the fifth question will be for somebody other than the participant to do something different, e.g. 'I would like them to ask if they can move my belongings.' It is worth pointing out that we do not have control over other people's behaviour towards us but we can control how we behave. In any given situation there is a choice of responses, some of which will support us in achieving the outcome we desire, others which will not. Many of the participants' usual behaviour patterns when their red flag is waved will be to 'react' as opposed to 'respond'. A reaction is something instant that happens automatically whereas a response is more controlled as time is taken to think about behaviour. Responding to a situation is far more likely to produce safety than reacting to it.

1.7 Sharks

Time: 10 min

Explanation

An energetic group game.

Intention

To act as a warm up, to begin to explore safety and danger and to practise working co-operatively.

Instructions

1. The facilitator sets out pieces of flip-chart paper at various points on the floor. There should be approximately one per four participants.

2. A volunteer is selected to be a shark. Everyone else is a swimmer. The pieces of paper represent islands where the swimmers are safe from the shark.

3. The participants move about the room until the facilitator calls 'shark'. At this point all the swimmers head for an island before the shark can touch them. Any swimmers that are touched become sharks.

4. After each round the facilitator should either remove a piece of flip-chart paper or tear them in half so that the safe space diminishes.

5. The game ends when there is only one swimmer left.

Exploration

- How did you find the game?

- How did it feel to be a swimmer?

- How did it feel to be a shark?

- How did it feel when there was less safe space?

- How did it feel when there were fewer swimmers left?

- What strategies did you use to keep yourself safe?

- Did you work as an individual or a team?

- Was there anything in this game that reminded you of real life?

Comments

This exercise provides the opportunity for participants to think about ways in which the gang can be both a source of safety and of danger. Being in a gang may provide safety as outsiders may be fearful of a large group. On the other hand if that gang is considered to be encroaching on another gang's territory this may lead to conflict. Furthermore, gang members caught alone or in small numbers by their rivals are at risk of harm.

1.8 FIDO

Time: 40 min

Explanation

A small groupwork exercise looking at relationships between facts and the interpretations we attach to these facts.

Intention

To explore how the interpretations we attach to incidents affect our actions.

Equipment

Four sets of seven FIDO cards (see pp.41–44).

Instructions

1. The facilitator asks their co-facilitator (or a volunteer) to sit still with their head in their hands, without other participants being aware of this instruction. They invite participants to say what is going on, e.g. the person is thinking, or they have a headache.

2. Once a range of suggestions has been written up on the flip chart the facilitator asks for the facts of what is happening, e.g. the person has their head in their hands, they are sitting down.

3. The facilitator explains that apart from the bare physical facts, everything else is a story made up by the observer. Their story is based on their interpretation of the facts, rather than the facts themselves. Stories are created because it helps to add meaning to a situation which is not fully understood. These stories are usually based on past experiences and therefore may not be useful to the current situation.

4. The facilitator then draws the following diagram on a piece of flip-chart paper.

Fact	Interpretations	Decision	Outcome

5. Next the facilitator gives an example of an incident in their personal life and breaks the incident down into fact, interpretation, decision and outcome:

- *Fact:* My friend did not return my telephone call for two days.

- *Interpretation:* They are ignoring me.

- *Decision:* Not to call them back.

- *Outcome:* We do not speak to each other for three weeks and the friendship is damaged.

6. The facilitator explains that the decision or action is based on the interpretation, not on the facts. They point out that it is not possible to change the facts of the situation but it is possible to change the interpretation of the facts, e.g. they did not receive my message. If the decision is based on our reaction the chances are we will not get the outcome we really want. Once you have a different interpretation you have more power and thus more choices.

7. The facilitator then splits the participants into groups of four. Each group is given a piece of flip-chart paper and seven cards. One fact card, two interpretation cards, two decision cards and two outcome cards.

8. The groups draw the above diagram on the flip-chart paper. They then look at their cards and decide which card fits in which box. The groups are aiming for two distinct logical stories based on different interpretations.

9. Once the groups have two stories they should make up a third alternative interpretation, decision and outcome.

10. The facilitator can ask whether they want to work through one of the group's real life situations. If they choose to do this, they will need to find a scenario that took place in which they didn't like the outcome.

Exploration

- Can we change the facts?

- How does our interpretation affect the outcome?

- What keeps us from changing our interpretations?

- What does that tell us about our relationship to conflict?

- What would it be like if we only made decisions based on the facts?

- How can we find out what is really happening?

Comments

An important feature of this exercise is supporting participants in being clear when they're extracting the facts of their own situations, e.g. one participant's fact was 'She gave me a dirty look.' In this instance a conversation took place in which it was discussed whether the dirty look was a fact or an interpretation of a fact. The fact in this situation is 'She looked at me,' and the dirty look is an interpretation. Other interpretations may be 'She squinted because the sun was in her eyes,' or 'She thought I was someone else.'

In certain situations a useful tool for extracting the facts is to have participants share the exact words that were spoken. So, instead of the fact being 'He disrespected me,' it becomes 'He said, "You're a tramp."' This allows for the participants to have a range of interpretations, e.g. 'He's disrespecting me,' 'He's trying to provoke me.' Many of the groups we have worked with have struggled with the notion of changing their interpretation. Even when we feel justified in our interpretation we can still construct a different interpretation which increases our choice of how to respond. For example, if someone says 'You're a tramp,' we can choose whether or not we're insulted. If the interpretation is 'He's trying to provoke me' and we feel attacked by that thought then the decision will necessarily be to attack back. If the interpretation is 'He's trying to provoke me' and the tone of the interpretation is one of realisation and understanding, then the decision can be 'I'm going to walk away.' In these instances it is important to reinforce that what really matters is the participant getting the outcome that they want.

FIDO cards

✂

Fact

A police officer stops you and asks if you are carrying any ID

Interpretation

He's stopping me because I'm black/Asian/young

Interpretation

The police are looking for someone who looks like me

Decision

Tell the police officer to mind his own business

Decision

Show the police officer any ID you have on you

Outcome

You are arrested

Outcome

You are thanked and you go on your way

FIDO cards

Fact

You are in a fast food restaurant and an adult comes in after you but gets served before you

---

Interpretation

They think they are better than me

Interpretation

They didn't notice I was first

Decision

Swear at them and tell them to wait until you have been served

Decision

Point out that you were in the queue first

Outcome

Have an argument and get refused service

Outcome

The other person apologises and you get served quickly

FIDO cards

Fact

Your friend has a spare ticket to see a concert and they invite another friend

Interpretation

They prefer the other person to me

Interpretation

My friend didn't know I liked the artist

Decision

Tell your friend that they are out of order

Decision

Tell your friend that you would have liked to have gone but you understand why they invited the other person

Outcome

Your friendship is damaged

Outcome

Your friend invites you the next time they have a spare ticket

✓

FIDO cards

Fact

Your friend tells you that they have a heard a rumour that you were beaten up by someone five years younger than you

Interpretation

Everyone is laughing at me

Interpretation

The person who told my friend the rumour wants me to get angry

Decision

Confront the person who your friend heard the rumour from

Decision

Tell your friend that you don't want to get involved in rumours

Outcome

You have a fight

Outcome

You do not hear any more rumours about yourself

1.9 24/7 Conflict Street

Time: 30 min

Explanation

A theoretical exercise looking at the cycle of attack and revenge between groups and the consequences of their actions.

Intention

To explore the costs and gains of group conflicts.

Instructions

1. Join some sheets of flip-chart paper together and draw a roundabout with seven roads leading off it, as shown in the diagram below.

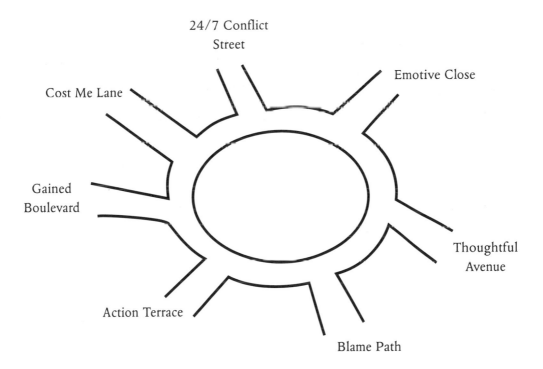

2. Participants will be asked to call out their responses to a series of questions as follows. The facilitator should write these words or phrases around the appropriate path.

Path 1: 24/7 Conflict Street

- Ask the participants: 'What conflict has your group been involved with? How did the conflict start?'

- Write their answers above the outside of the first street. Explain: 'When all these things happened, it was because…' – e.g. 'Mustapha stole the girlfriend of one of our crew.'

Path 2: Emotive Close

- Ask the participants: 'How did you feel when all this happened?'

- Call out specific examples from the first path and get responses to some of these – e.g. 'angry', 'excited', 'sad', 'depressed'.

Path 3: Thoughtful Avenue

- Ask the participants: 'What did you think when this happened to you/to one of you?' 'What thoughts did you have when…' (use an example from 24/7 Conflict Street) – e.g. 'They can't do that to us; who do they think they are?'

Path 4: Blame Path

- Ask the participants: 'Who or what is to blame for what happened?' Call out specific examples from Path 1 and ask 'What thoughts did you have about who was to blame?' – e.g. 'They made us do it – they're always starting.'

- The facilitator inputs that we may feel we have been 'done to' and that we are victims of circumstance.

Path 5: Action Terrace

- Ask the participants: 'What do you do when these things happen to you and you experience these feelings? What action do you take when you have these thoughts?' – e.g. 'take drugs', 'become violent', 'get back-up', 'carry a weapon', 'steal'.

- The facilitator inputs that when these things happen to us, our thoughts and feelings can lead us to want something in order to get revenge, to get our own back.

Path 6: Gained Boulevard

- Ask the participants: 'What did you gain for yourself?' 'What do you gain for others/when you took one of these actions?'

- Call out specific words written near Path 5 and get responses – e.g. 'satisfaction', 'power', 'respect'.

Path 7: Cost Me Lane

- Ask the participants: 'What did you lose/what did it cost you when you took one of these actions?'

- Again, call out specific words from Path 5.

3.　Ask the participants if there are places on the roundabout where the group could do something differently which would stop them going round and round: 'Where are they?' 'What would it take to do that?'

Exploration

- How old is our vicious cycle?

- At what point in the cycle does the danger escalate?

- What is the safest point of the cycle?

- Where do we have choices?

- When do we normally get off our vicious cycle?

- How would reinterpreting what we think affect the costs and gains?

Comments

Below is an example of running this exercise with a gang of 18-year-old men who had been in conflict with a rival gang for the previous six years.

Path 1: 24/7 Conflict Street

　'When we were 12 Mustapha stole the girlfriend of one of our crew.'

Path 2: Emotive Close

　'We felt angry.'

Path 3: Thoughtful Avenue

　'We thought that Mustapha was deliberately trying to disrespect our friend and we weren't going to let him get away with this.'

Path 4: Blame Path

　'Mustapha is taking liberties.'

Path 5: Action Terrace

　'We went over to his area and beat him up.'

Path 6: Gained Boulevard

　'We gained status and felt that we had protected our friend.'

Path 7: Cost Me Lane

> 'It cost us our sense of safety as we knew that Mustapha and his crew would come for revenge.'

> 'Mustapha and five of his crew caught two of our crew and beat them up.'

With this group the cycle continued for six years and at the time we were working with them Mustapha was recovering from spending two weeks in a coma having been hit with a baseball bat. Two members of the other gang were arrested and sentenced for the attack. The group was struck by the cyclical nature of the conflict and how events had spiralled so that the costs of their actions had increased whilst the gains of their actions had decreased. This led into a discussion about what could happen now to break the vicious cycle.

1.10 Blame Game

Time: 15 min

Explanation

A whole group game exploring blame.

Intention

To recognise the value of taking responsibility for our actions.

Instructions

1. The game starts with the facilitator who blames the person to their left for something simple, e.g. being late.

2. The person who is being blamed justifies what they did and blames the person to their left, e.g. 'It wasn't my fault – they were supposed to phone me and wake me but they never did.'

3. This continues around the circle until everybody has had a go.

Exploration

- How did it feel to be blamed?

- What are your thoughts when you are blamed for something?

- Are people familiar with blame and justification?

- Why do we do it?

- What are the outcomes of blaming someone else?

- What is the impact of blame on ourselves/others?

- What would happen if we took responsibility for our actions?

- What would be the outcomes of taking responsibility?

Comments

It is important in this exercise to make the distinction between 'shouldering the blame' and 'taking responsibility'. When we shoulder or avoid blame we are either justifying our actions with reasons as we feel we are in the right, or we are blaming ourselves or others for things going wrong. Taking responsibility is when we are willing to take responsibility for our actions and for the consequences of those actions whether or not we could have predicted them.

One group we worked with returned 20 minutes late from their lunch break. They explained that they were late because they didn't like the food that was provided so they went to a takeaway which took a long time to prepare their food. We put it to the group that this may well be true but it was still an excuse. The group could not necessarily have predicted that it would take a long time to prepare the food, but if they were taking responsibility they may have kept an eye on the time, asked for an estimate of when the food would be ready, rung ahead to let the facilitators know the problems they were having, cancelled the order and gone somewhere else, or taken a whole other range of actions so that they could ensure that they would be back on time. If we had told the group that if they returned on time we would give them a cash reward we were certain that participants would have taken responsibility and returned on time.

Taking responsibility is being aware of your 'ability to respond' to situations in a way that is more likely to get you a constructive outcome. Sometimes when we say a situation is out of our control it is patently is not the case.

1.11 Choices And Consequences

Time: 45 min

Explanation

A group exercise in which options in a potential situation of conflict are generated and explored.

Intention

To develop choices and explore consequences when confronted with potentially violent situations.

Instructions

1. A volunteer is selected from the group to act out a narrated scene. They are told that the facilitator will read out six stage directions for them to follow. The volunteer is asked to follow instructions and is assured that they will not be asked to do anything silly or embarrassing.

2. The facilitator sets up the stage and reads out the instructions:

    - A young man is sitting at home watching television.
    - His mobile phone rings.
    - He picks it up and answers it.
    - He talks for a short while and then hangs up.
    - He goes into the kitchen and gets a knife.
    - He puts the knife inside his jacket and runs out of the house.

3. The audience is asked what they think is happening, e.g. Who might this person be? What do they think the person on the other end of the phone is saying? Where do they think the young man is going? The facilitator should try and draw out the scenario that would involve a young man being called to provide back-up to his friends in a gang fight. The audience is then asked to explore what they think the character might be thinking and feeling at different points in the scene.

4. Now the audience is asked to think about what might have happened to lead up to the mobile phone ringing and what could be the possible consequences of the young man leaving the house with a knife. Both positive and negative consequences are explored. A scenario should be agreed on.

5. Another volunteer is selected from the audience. This volunteer will play the role of the person making the phone call. The two volunteers are given two minutes to rehearse the conversation.

6. The narrated scene is re-enacted, this time incorporating the phone call.

7. The audience is told they will see the scene for a final time. This time they can stop the action at any point they feel something different could happen. When an audience member stops the action they are invited to offer their suggestion as to what could happen. The facilitator will take responsibility for fielding this process. If appropriate, the facilitator may ask an audience member to take one of the volunteer's positions to try out their strategy. When the narrated scene is re-enacted it is possible to have a variety of endings based on the suggestions from the audience.

8. The facilitator asks who is responsible for making the choices in this scenario. The facilitator should input that by making choices we are responsible for the consequences, even if they are not what we intended.

Exploration

- When are the moments of safety in this scenario?
- When are the moments of danger?
- How was change effected?
- Did the changes to the character mean they fared better or worse?
- How might the characters' choices affect their future relationship with the group?
- Did changes to one character force the other to adapt?
- What is the impact of choice?
- How is this exercise relevant to real life?

Comments

At the heart of this exercise is the concept of thinking through the potential consequences of choices. When participants are asked why they behaved in a certain way a common response is 'I had no choice.' This exercise helps to demonstrate that there are always choices, even though these choices may feel limited. For example, in the narrated scene, if the character chooses not to back up their friend there is a multitude of possible consequences, e.g. they may not be backed up in the future, they may be ostracised, they may be respected for standing their ground. If the character chooses to back up their friend they may get hurt, arrested or respected. The hope is that by exploring the potential costs and gains of each choice the participants will be in a stronger position to make informed decisions about their behaviour. When situations similar to this arise they will have already thought through the possible consequences and they can then respond rather than react. The very process of participating in this exercise provides a group with the opportunity to hear their peers share their feelings around these complex issues. It is useful to point out to the groups that if any participants are considering changing their behaviour it can be helpful to have conversations about this with their peers prior to the request for support. For strategies aimed at managing potentially difficult conversations see the Boxing Ring exercise (p.102).

Chapter 2
Space and Territory

When you go to different manors you get people looking at you, like screwing [to give a bad look]; and you feel a bit shaky. When you're around your own area as next boys coming through its like 'why are you trying to walk through my area like you're something big?' But when you're with your boys and a next set of boys come into the area, you see them with their head down, they won't be screwing you.

If you go New Cross, and you are Somalian, they think that you are a Woolwich Boy and that you are up to something. They beat you up for no reason.

Participants from Leap's action research project

At an early age children begin to learn about space and territory. In the interests of safety, limits are set for where children can safely go and whom they can talk to. Territory goes beyond a geographical space and becomes a reflection of values and worth. For example, parents may allow their child to go alone to a certain area they consider safe. Borders and territories protect from others, act as a foundation and give strength. The safe space can range from a set of streets to a building to a bed.

Most gangs operate within clearly defined territories and a rival gang entering this space is viewed as a deliberate provocation. With gangs, the ownership is purely notional, as they have no legal rights to the areas they lay claim to. In claiming these spaces, young people are able to make a space their own and experience a sense of belonging, culture, kinship and history. Some gangs' territories include local amenities such as a youth centre or shopping precinct, which makes it difficult for members of other gangs to access these resources. One gang member told us that in order to go to the doctor's surgery he needed to enter another gang's territory. The safest time for him to go there was early in the morning, before the enemy group had the opportunity to form for the day.

Many young people hang out on the street because they think there is nothing else for them to do. Although they may not be deliberately marking their territory, the message interpreted by outsiders is that the neighbourhood is at best unwelcoming and at worst frightening. It is no coincidence that most gang conflict takes place in summer when young people are outdoors.

Often drug dealing is not related to territory. There may well be a drug gang operating in an area where several territorial gangs are involved in conflict. These drug gangs exist separately from the territorial conflicts and tend not to get involved in them as this narrows the market and thus the financial return.

Some spaces are communal safe spaces. Young people from rival gangs may attend the same school and often there will be an unspoken rule that gang conflict will not take place on the school site. In other situations sworn enemies become allies. Gangs from an estate on the outskirts of a major city may be locked in conflict until they enter the city. If a conflict arises whilst in the city these rivalries sometimes disperse and the group fight as a unit. This fluidity to gang conflict is similar to the partisan fighting that takes place amongst football hooligans.

Key questions

This chapter encourages participants to ask:

- What space can I call my own?

- Who controls these streets?

Aims

- To look at unwritten rules that relate to territory.

- To explore the concept of personal and local territory.

- To examine the existing conflicts in a particular local area.

Space and Territory Day Plan

Day Intro	10.00	5 min
Gathering – Something I like about my area	10.05	10 min
Game – Territories Game	10.15	15 min
Conflict Maps	10.30	50 min
BREAK	11.20	20 min
Game – 1 To 11	11.40	10 min
Country Map	11.50	15 min
Small Group Discussion	12.05	20 min
Where Am I From?	12.25	20 min
Personal Space	12.45	15 min
LUNCH	1.00	60 min
Gathering – Think of a time when you've been somewhere you didn't feel welcome	2.00	10 min
Game – Walking Trust Circle	2.10	20 min
Gangs In Your Area	2.30	60 min
BREAK	3.30	20 min
Game – Pulse Train	3.50	10 min
Chain Reaction	4.00	50 min
Close – Something you're looking forward to doing this evening	4.50	10 min

2.1 Territories Game

Time: 15 min

Explanation

An active game in which two teams compete for group size and territory.

Intention

To explore feelings around having territory encroached upon and switching sides.

Instructions

1. The room is set up so that tables are turned on their sides to act as barricades.

2. The participants are asked to select two leaders who then each select a team from the remainder of the group. Both groups will begin the game hidden behind the barricades.

3. Each group is instructed that they will be given four soft balls, which they should throw at the other team. If a member of the other team is hit they then join the thrower's team. If the leader of a team is hit, then they must select someone from their team to join the other team.

4. When one team is much larger than the other team, the facilitator should stop the game and explain that the smaller team should move their barricades back one metre and the larger team should move theirs forward. The facilitator continues to do this as the sides change.

5. The facilitator should choose an appropriate time for the game to finish.

Exploration

- Did you like the game?

- What did you like about it?

- How were your leaders selected?

- What was it like to be picked first/last?

- How did it feel when you were winning/losing?

- How did it feel when you swapped sides?

- Did it feel different when your team leader asked you to swap sides?

- How did you feel when you were gaining/losing territory?

- How close is this game to real life?

- How did you feel at the end?

- When things got very heated in the game, were you reacting or responding?

- How might this relate to a real life situation where you are involved in a dispute over territory?

- How quickly are you making decisions?

Comments

The territories game can produce a range of emotions connected with gang conflict. Many groups become highly excited in this game. It is interesting to explore with the group the effects of this excitement in terms of how it may impact on their behaviour and their willingness to take risks in the moment when involved in conflicts. It is important to acknowledge with young people just how important the buzz of adrenalin is to them and it may be useful to discuss other activities which may create that buzz without some of the associated risk.

2.2 Conflict Maps

Time: 50 min

Explanation

A small group exercise in which young people draw maps of their local area highlighting where and when conflict occurs.

Intention

To explore the relationship between space and conflict and examine the existing conflicts in a particular local area.

Instructions

1. The participants are divided into groups of two or three. Each group is given two pieces of flip-chart paper and pen.

2. Each group is asked to draw a bird's eye map of their local area, marking down the places where conflicts take place.

3. Once they have drawn the maps the groups answer the following questions:

   - Where do the biggest conflicts happen?

   - When conflict happens, where would you be?

   - Once you are in that area, what are the unwritten rules?

4. Each group then draws a time line on their map to show when the conflicts happen. This could be a 24-hour clock and days of the week or it could be historical.

5. The groups then identify on the maps where resources are located, e.g. shops, youth facilities, sports centre, doctors' surgeries, etc.

6. Each group is given the opportunity to show their picture to the larger group.

Exploration

- Did you notice anything different about your area?

- Are there particular reasons why conflicts take place in certain areas?

- Is there any safe space?

- Are there any safe times?

- Is there a relationship between territory and resources?

- If your rival group/gang drew a map of the area how do you think it would be similar/different?

- What choices does having done the map give you?

Working with two antagonistic groups

- How are the maps similar?

- How are they different?

- Are you surprised at how the other group view their/your territory?

Comments

When bringing two or more antagonistic groups together this exercise can be used in the early stages to explore their perspectives on the same geographical area. The maps can create commonality, as the gangs will be able to see where their maps are similar and where they are different. It may be that the maps show certain areas where there are common enemies for both groups. The danger of this is that the groups will be sharing sensitive information which, if used by their rivals in the wrong way, could result in injury. Further discussion relating to the careful planning around bringing rival groups together can be found in 'How to Use this Manual' (p.13).

2.3 1 To 11

Time: 10 min

Explanation

A whole group teamwork game in which the participants attempt to count to 11.

Intention

To explore feelings around working as a team.

Instructions

The aim is for all the participants to count to 11 saying one number at a time, without deciding who says which number. Every time two or more people say the same number at the same time you go back to the beginning again.

Exploration

- Did you like the game?
- How did it feel when you had to go back to the beginning?
- Was it always different people saying the numbers?
- How did it feel when you got to 11/a high number?
- Did everyone join in?
- What strategies did you use to support the process?
- Is the game like real life in any way?

Comments

This game requires participants to rely on a different set of communication skills that they will generally use. Encourage participants to steer clear of obvious strategies such as nodding to each other, or going around in a circle. Ask them to see if they can simply sense when someone else is about to speak. By focusing and acutely concentrating they will become aware of when to speak and when not to speak. It is an opportunity to focus on different ways in which the group can work well together. Groups and gangs of young people often seem to have the ability to think with a 'group mind', i.e. to make decisions about a course of action almost without speaking about it. It is one of the phenomena of group or gang behaviour that can seem most impenetrable to workers. A further development of this exercise could be to explore the 'group mind' more extensively with participants. What are the situations where the 'group mind' takes over? What are the underlying thoughts or beliefs that allow a 'group mind' to operate?

2.4 Country Map

Time: 15 min

Explanation

A whole group exercise in which participants are asked to identify different parts of the country they live in and their relationship to these places.

Intention

To explore issues of belonging.

Instructions

1. The facilitator explains that the room represents a map of the country. The top end of the room represents the north, the bottom end represents the south, the right side of the room represents the east and the left side represents the west.

2. The participants are then asked to place themselves on the map according to the following questions:

    -   Where was the first place you lived in this country? (If the majority of the group first lived in the same town then they should arrange themselves according to what part of the town they were born in.)

    -   Where do you live now?

    -   Go to a place where you have a relative living.

    -   Go to a place where you've been and you think nobody else may have been to.

    -   Go to a place where you have a friend.

    -   Where are you now?

    At each question the participants should be stopped and different people asked to explain why they are where they are.

Exploration

-   Did anyone learn anything new about anybody in the group?

-   Did anyone ask someone else where they were in order to gauge where they should stand?

-   Did anyone feel that someone else in the group was in the wrong place?

-   How did that feel?

- What stories do you have about people from other places?

- Where do you feel you belong?

Comments

When working with gangs that have a history of immigration this exercise can be changed so the map is a world map. It is also particularly useful when working with gangs that are in conflict and come from different ethnicities as they get to learn a little bit more about each other. When running this exercise with two rival gangs, one of African Caribbean heritage and the other of Somali heritage, it emerged from several of the Somali young people that they first emigrated to other North European countries. Due to intense experiences of racism and lack of proximity to a mosque their families had relocated to the UK. On arriving in the UK the group reported a sense of relief and happiness at seeing so many people from a variety of cultures. This quickly turned to despair when they realised that many of the young people at their schools treated them with disdain, in particular that many of the African Caribbean young people did not view the Somali young people as 'black'.

2.5 Small Group Discussion

Time: 20 min

Explanation

A small group exercise in which the participants are invited to explore a range of themes related to space and territory.

Intention

To challenge thinking about space and territory and generate discussion.

Instructions

1. The facilitator divides the group into five equal-sized groups. Each group is given one of the following statements to discuss for five minutes:

    - So long as I'm in my territory, I'll be safe.

    - If you enter your enemy's territory they have the right to attack you.

    - Young people take pride in their local area.

    - Some young people can go to whichever area they like.

    - Drug dealing and gang territory are directly linked.

2. Each small group then feeds back to the large group. The rest of the participants are then invited to comment on the issue.

Exploration

- If everyone agrees, does it make it a good idea?

- Why do you think people from the same area hold different perspectives?

Comments

It is interesting to explore the question around the gang's safety in their own area. Groups have fed back to us that while they feel safest in their own area because they can easily access back-up, their area can also present a danger as rival groups know where to find them. Some gangs have told us that the centre of town is often a safe space as it is neutral.

2.6 Where Am I From?

Time: 20 min

Explanation

A paired sharing exercise in which participants tell their partner about themselves and the environment they grew up in.

Intention

To explore the influences of environment on growing up.

Instructions

1. The chairs are set up in two circles, one inside the other. The chairs in the outer circle should be opposite and facing the chairs in the inner circle. The facilitator asks the participants to choose a chair.

2. The pairs are then asked to spend a few minutes sharing their thoughts with their partner on the first of the following questions.

3. After two or three minutes the facilitator stops the conversations and asks the participants in the outer circle to move one chair to their right. The new pairs then begin discussing the second question. This format continues until all the questions have been answered.

Questions

- Did you move much as a child?
- Did you enjoy school?
- Did you have family living close by?
- Was where you lived a rich or poor area?
- Were there people from lots of different cultures in your area?
- Was there much violence in the area?

Exploration

- How did it feel to be listened to?
- How did it feel to listen?
- What common ground did you find with your partner?

- How does where we come from affect us?

- If we change our environment what else can change?

Comments

Previous experiences running this exercise have led to interesting nature vs. nurture debates. The environment that participants come from undoubtedly affects their character. However, they are also responsible for the choices they make in their lives. These choices will reflect how participants perceive themselves and what choices they need to make to take a lead in their life. In extreme cases participants have talked about the need to leave their town as they feel that, even if they make a choice to stop being involved in violent gang activity, their rivals will still be out to get them.

2.7 Personal Space

Time: 15 min

Explanation

A whole group exercise exploring different perspectives.

Intention

To explore feelings and attitudes about personal space.

Instructions

1. The facilitator attaches nine pieces of flip-chart paper together so they form one larger piece of paper. They draw the following diagram on the paper.

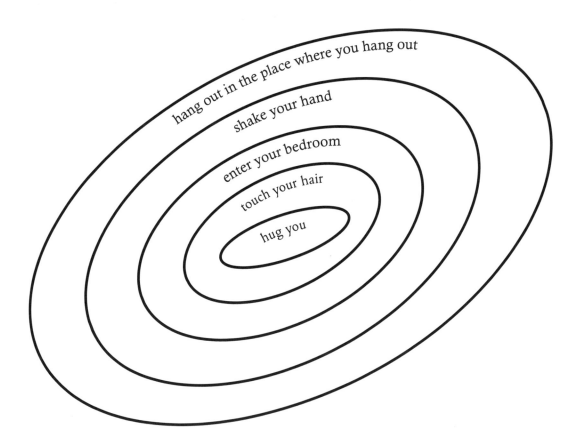

2. The facilitator explains that they are going to read out six different character parts. These characters are: family member, police officer, someone you're attracted to, rival gang member, stranger, closest friend.

3.   When the characters are read out the participants decide how close they would want to be to that person and they go and stand in that circle on the flip-chart paper. For example, if a participant feels it is acceptable for a family member to hug them they should stand in the inner circle.

Exploration

- Why is it OK for certain people to behave in one way towards you but not for others?

- How do you feel if your personal space is invaded?

- What can you do about this?

Comments

Depending on the size of the group, issues around personal space may arise in the process of this exercise, as several participants will want to stand in the same circle on the flip-chart paper. It is important to be mindful of cultural/gender differences as being physically close to each other may have different meaning for participants.

2.8 Walking Trust Circle

Time: 20 min

Explanation

A group trust exercise.

Intention

To create an atmosphere of trust and to explore the issue of trust.

Instructions

1. The participants stand up in a circle. The facilitator explains that this is a trust exercise and it is important for everyone on the outside of the circle to behave in a way that supports the participant in the middle having the best experience possible of the exercise.

2. One of the facilitators demonstrates this exercise by standing in the centre of the circle with their eyes closed and their arms folded across their chest.

3. The other facilitator guides the person in the centre of the circle towards the perimeter. When they reach the wall of the circle the participant gently redirects them into the circle.

4. Once a few participants have had a go, ask a volunteer to walk without a guide.

5. If appropriate the facilitator can silently signal to the participants to make the circle bigger or smaller.

6. The facilitator should encourage everyone to have a go.

Exploration

- How did it feel to be in the middle?
- When you were in the middle what did you need in order to take part in the exercise?
- How did it feel to be on the outside?
- How easy/hard was it to trust others?
- Who do you trust?
- Did anyone feel totally safe?
- Did anyone open their eyes?
- How did it feel when the circle changed size?

- Where in the circle did you feel most safe?

- Where, in general, do you feel most safe?

- Is there anyone in the group you felt unsafe around?

- When do you trust blindly?

- What was it like to feel trusted?

Comments

If working with a particularly lively group it might be useful as part of the first instruction to do some preliminary exploration of what behaviour might help someone feel safe in the middle of the circle and what behaviour might cause them to feel unsafe. It is also sometimes useful to point out that everyone who steps into the middle is taking a risk and to ask participants to think through how they would like to be supported when taking a risk or trying something unfamiliar or new.

Participants may find they trust some members of the group more than others in this exercise. This can lead into discussion exploring who in the group participants might trust with different things: for instance, who they would trust with a secret, who they would lend something to, whose advice they would trust, who they would trust to support them when in trouble. Vocalising the different levels of trust a group feel for each other can be a difficult experience for some participants but it will help them in knowing what to expect from each other.

2.9 Gangs In Your Area

Time: 60 min

Explanation

Tableau work exploring the characteristics of gangs in a particular area.

Intention

To reflect on how participants see gangs in their area and how they would like things to be.

Instructions

1. Ask participants to get into groups of four. In their groups the participants devise three still images:

    (a) What is it that gangs in your area do?

    (b) How does this affect you?

    (c) How would you like it to be?

2. The group show back their images and give a title to each picture.

3. As each image is given a title the facilitator writes the titles on a piece of flip-chart paper.

4. Once all the images have been shown back the facilitator explores each set of images with the participants by wordstorming what would need to happen to go from tableau (a) to tableau (c).

Exploration

-   What were the similarities/differences between the images?

-   Do you relate to the gangs in the images?

-   How realistic were the images in tableau (c)?

-   Who or what needs to change to achieve tableau (c)?

Comments

For facilitators who are experienced in facilitating tableau this exercise can be developed by asking the participants to move slowly from tableau (a) to tableau (c). After they have moved, participants can be asked to think about what needed to happen to their feelings, thoughts and actions to make this move. On several occasions when running this exercise, tableau (c) has shown rival groups shaking hands. In order to reality check this possibility participants can be asked to imagine themselves shaking hands and think about what that might feel like. They can also be asked how long it might take to achieve this level of reconciliation and what steps they would need to take to make this practically possible.

A fascinating experience of this exercise took place during a residential trip with five gangs from different parts of the UK. At this time there had been lots of media interest in African Caribbean gangs due to recent murders in Birmingham. The two African Caribbean groups from Birmingham and Manchester showed their images of drug dealing, car jacking and violence. When it was the turn of the gang from Northern Ireland to show their images their first tableau image was a scene involving paramilitaries called 'No Surrender' and their final tableau image was of Protestants and Catholics drinking in the same pub. When asked about moving from tableau (a) to tableau (c) they talked about the need for mass re-education, decommissioning of weapons and a renewed attempt at the peace process. There was a sense of shock from those watching that the levels of violence experienced by the Northern Irish gang were so intense. Members of the four other gangs were not aware of the day-to-day realities for young people in Northern Ireland and were surprised by the details of their experiences.

2.10 Pulse Train

Time: 10 min

Explanation

A whole group game involving physical contact.

Intention

To explore reactions.

Instructions

1. The participants sit around a table with their hands shoulder-width apart. Each participant's right hand should be within an inch of the participant to their right's left hand.

2. The facilitator starts the pulse train by tapping their right hand and then their left hand on the table. The person immediately to their left continues by tapping their right hand and then their left hand on the table. This action continues round the circle.

3. After two circuits the facilitator warns that anyone who doesn't respond immediately to the pulse is out.

4. The facilitator then introduces the rule that if they tap their hand on the table twice, the pulse then changes direction. At this point the facilitator is the only person who can change direction. Once the participants get used to the new rule anyone can change direction.

5. The game continues until two people are left in.

Exploration

- Did you like the game?

- How did it feel when you were out?

- How easy/difficult was it to react when someone changed the direction?

- Why? Did anyone think they were unfairly judged as being out?

- How did you respond to this?

- Did your response make a difference?

- Is there anything else you could have done?

Comments

Participants' attention can be drawn towards thinking about how their reactions affected others in the game. In particular, if any of the participants felt they were unfairly judged as being out, their reaction would have affected others in the group. If a table is not available for this exercise, participants can be asked to hold hands or wrists (depending on how comfortable they are with physical touch) and squeeze the next person's hand or wrist.

2.11 Chain Reaction

Time: 50 min

Explanation

A role-play exercise exploring the possible reasons behind a violent incident.

Intention

To uncover the causal sequence behind a seemingly random act of violence. To explore the motives behind the act. To look for alternatives to violent behaviour.

Instructions

1. The facilitator asks the group for five or six volunteers. The first volunteer takes up a frozen image in the circle as though they were just about to strike somebody.

2. The second volunteer then places themselves in the action in relation to the first volunteer's position, e.g. they might choose to show a frozen image of someone striking back. This continues until all the volunteers have taken a position in the frozen image.

3. The facilitator then invites the volunteers and the rest of the participants to make up a story about the scene. The participants decide: the names of the first two volunteers, who everyone else is, where it is happening and why it is happening. As the story is being devised the facilitator fills in the Scene 3 box of the following chart, which the facilitator had previously drawn on a flip chart.

Scene 1	**Scene 2**
Who?	Who?
Where?	Where?
Why?	Why?
Scene 3	**Scene 4**
Who?	Who?
Where?	Where?
Why?	Why?

4. The facilitator then asks the participants what might have happened two hours earlier that led up to the incident. Once a story has been agreed on the facilitator fills in Scene 2.

5. Next the facilitator asks the participants what might have happened on the morning of the incident. This time the facilitator fills in Scene 1.

6. Finally the participants agree on a possible outcome for the story and this is put in Scene 4.

7. The participants are then split into four smaller groups and each group is asked to make a role-play of a scene.

8. In their small groups the participants should recap the basics of the story. Once this has happened the participants should divide up the roles and prepare the role-play.

9. Once the groups are ready they show back their scenes in chronological order.

10. After each scene has been shown back the facilitator then asks the participants the following questions:

    - Who has been affected?

    - How?

    - How do you think the characters feel?

    - How can the harm be put right?

    - What made the situation get worse?

    - Who could have made a difference?

    - How would that have affected the following scene?

11. The facilitator then inputs that when a situation gets worse it is known as escalating and when it gets better it is known as de-escalating.

12. The facilitator then asks the participants to return to their smaller groups and gives them each a copy of the escalate/de-escalate diagram. Each group thinks about the scene they role-played and decides on three things that made the situation escalate and three things that could have made the situation de-escalate. These are then written on the flip chart.

Exploration

- Who did you identify most with in each of the scenes?

- Who did you identify with least?

- Why?

- What did the bystanders contribute to the conflict?

- At what points did the conflict escalate?

- At what points could someone have given a different response which would have de-escalated the conflict?

- What happens to the choices people have available to them as the conflict escalates?

Comments

This is an example of what a group might come up with as a possible scenario. In this case the scenario that the participants came up with was part of a school setting.

Scene 1:   *Tony shouts at his mum.*

Who?   Tony, his mum, two younger sisters.

Where?   At home.

Why?   Tony's mum does not have enough money to give him for lunch.

Scene 2:   *A group of students are laughing at Tony.*

Who?   Peter, John, Tony, various onlookers.

Where?   School corridor.

Why?   Peter and John are messing around. John pushes Peter onto Tony.

Scene 3:   *Tony is about to punch John.*

Who?   Tony, John, various onlookers.

Where?   In the school playground.

Why?   Tony feels humiliated and angry.

Scene 4:   *Tony is being excluded.*

Who?   Tony, Peter, head teacher.

Where?   Head teacher's office.

Why?   Tony broke John's nose.

Escalating the situation

1.   Tony shouts at his mum.

2.   John pushes Peter.

3.   Onlookers laugh at Tony.

De-escalating the situation

1. Tony does not shout at his mum.

2. John and Peter apologise to Tony.

3. Onlookers don't get involved.

Escalate/De-escalate Diagram

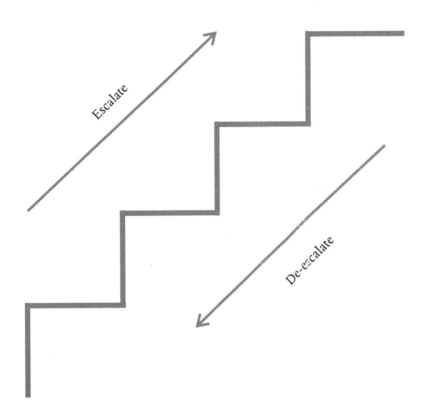

Chapter 3

Status and Reputation

If you want to be famous, you've got to be talented – if you want to be the toughest you have to join a gang. Young people go to jail: some of them want to for status.

Participant from Leap's action research project

The acquisition of status is the driving force of many societies. Social status denotes the relative position of a person on a recognised scale of social worth. It may be inherited or acquired and can change during a lifetime. Acquiring high status through legitimate means often involves educational, occupational or financial success. Young people in gangs tend to leave school with few or no qualifications, which severely limits their ability to attain status through traditional routes. In response to limited access to conventional means for attaining status, membership of a gang can provide an alternative means of attaining status because value is assigned to behaviour that is criminal and considered to be dangerous or detrimental by the wider society.

The lawbreaking behaviour of gang members is more openly visible than that of non-gang members, e.g. graffiti, large group fights. This is attributed to a desire to communicate a particular impression to fellow gang members and wider society. This behaviour enables gang members to acquire recognition within their community and with that increase their sense of self-worth.

Within gangs each member will have also have a different status level. Status is bestowed for different things, e.g. being the best fighter, joker, having the most money. It can also be gained by being close to someone who has high status, e.g. good friends with someone who has a reputation for violence, parents who are held in high regard in the community.

Reputation is closely linked to the notion of status. Reputation is the story that is created about the status of individuals and groups; it can be a mixture of fact and fiction. The individual gang member may then make decisions that will either reinforce or repudiate their reputation. A gang's reputation acts like a magnet attracting a range of reactions from other gangs, groups, the police, the media and the local community. This reputation may then become a self-fulfilling prophecy as gang members are under pressure to behave in the way that is expected of them.

Regardless of status, there are always choices available in situations of conflict and these choices bring power to individuals. The power to make choices may increase with high status. However, this does not mean that having low status results in not being powerful because choice is available to everyone, regardless of their position. Ultimately, it is the choices that individuals make which will impact on their status and reputation.

Key questions

This chapter encourages participants to ask themselves:

- How do I gain status and recognition in my life?

- What power do I have?

Aims

- To explore the concept of status.

- To look at what we have done to gain or lose status.

- To understand how a group's reputation is formed.

- To explore the difference between how we see ourselves and how we are seen by others.

- To look at the concept of power and how this links to status and reputation.

Status and Reputation Day Plan

Day Intro	10.00	5 min
Gathering – Something that you have achieved in your life	10.05	10 min
Game – Howdy Status	10.15	10 min
Wordstorm – What is Status?	10.25	10 min
Sinking Ships	10.35	15 min
Status And Power	10.50	20 min
Taking A Risk	11.10	20 min
BREAK	11.30	20 min
Second Guessing	11.50	15 min
Myths	12.05	55 min
LUNCH	1.00	60 min
Gathering – One thing that has had a powerful impact on my life	2.00	10 min
Game – Jailbreak	2.10	15 min
I've Got The Power	2.25	20 min
The Powerful And The Powerless	2.45	35 min
BREAK	3.20	20 min
Push Me If You Can	3.40	15 min
Boxing Ring	3.55	60 min
Close	4.55	5 min

3.1 Howdy Status

Time: 10 min

Explanation

A physical whole group exercise.

Intention

To explore the choice and challenges we face when dealing with status.

Instructions

1.   The facilitator asks everyone to stand in a circle making sure that there is enough space behind them for someone to run around the circle.

2.   A volunteer stands on the outside of the circle. Their aim is to take someone's place in the circle.

3.   The volunteer moves around the outside of the circle choosing someone to race against.

4.   Once they have chosen their opponent they tap them lightly on the shoulder. Both participants then race around the circle in opposite directions. When they meet they greet each other by shaking hands and saying 'Howdy, Howdy, Howdy'. They cannot let go of each other's hand until they have finished saying the phrase.

5.   They then continue running round the circle as fast as they can until one of them gets into the empty space left behind. Participants are not allowed to run through the circle, hold on to anyone or trip each other.

6.   The facilitator chooses for the game to finish when everyone has had a go.

Exploration

*   How did you find that game?

*   What was your decision to choose your opponent based on?

*   Who picked someone they thought they would be able to win against?

*   Who picked someone because it would be a challenge to win against them?

*   Who picked someone for fun?

*   What was it like facing someone who you thought was faster than you?

*   Was there anyone you thought was faster than you that you actually beat?

*   Was there anyone you thought was not faster than you that beat you?

- What does this tell us about status and the way we challenge people who have equal, lower or higher status than ourselves?

- What kind of tactics and strategies did people use?

- Did anyone's status change in the process of playing the game?

Comments

The facilitator may need to give a definition of status if participants aren't clear what it means or how the concept relates to the game. To use this game to explore status, the facilitator will need to let it carry on for a bit so participants can have several goes at running round the circle. As the game progresses participants will become more engaged and may use a range of manipulative tactics to 'win'. When our status in a group is threatened we may lie, cheat, create a distraction, pick on someone who is weaker than us or blame someone else. None of these tactics are necessarily wrong in themselves, it is just interesting to see the lengths we will go to when we feel our status in a group is under threat.

3.2 What Is Status?

Time: 10 min

Explanation

A whole group wordstorm exercise.

Intention

To explore the concept of status.

Instructions

1. The facilitator writes the word 'status' in the middle of a piece of flip-chart paper. Participants are invited to respond to the following four questions:

   - What is status?

   - Who has status?

   - How do you get status?

   - Where do you have status?

2. The facilitator writes the responses to the four questions in different colours on the flip chart.

Exploration

- Can the same person have high status in one situation and low status in another?

- What does high status give us?

- What does low status give us?

- How does our level of status affect us?

- Is it possible to change your status?

- How can you do this?

Comments

The group might need prompting in answering some of these questions and therefore the facilitator may want to think through possible responses in preparation. It is interesting for the group to think about who gives status: for instance, a police officer and a good fighter both have high status in some situations and low status in others. People attribute status to others for different reasons and group members could be encouraged to think about why they give particular people high or low status.

3.3 Sinking Ships

Time: 15 min

Explanation

An interactive group exercise using role-play to explore how status can be gained or lost.

Intention

To gain an insight into the wide variety of responses to status and to explore how status can be gained or lost depending on the context.

Equipment

Character cards (see p.85).

Instructions

1. Participants sit in a circle or in the shape of a ship.

2. Each participant is given a prepared card with a role on it and is told not to share the information with the other participants unless they feel it would benefit them.

3. The facilitator tells the participants that they are all on board a ship that is sinking. The ship will go down in ten minutes. There is one lifeboat that has space for five people.

4. Each of the participants puts forward reasons why they should be allowed to be saved. By the end of the ten minutes the group should have agreed on who is going in the lifeboat. The reasons given can be connected to their role or status, e.g. skills, personal responsibility, age. If anyone wants to volunteer to stay on the ship they can. The facilitator can choose whether or not they take a character card. Their role is to facilitate the decision-making process.

5. After ten minutes the facilitator asks the participants for their decision. If they have not come to a conclusion they all show their cards and vote on who gets into the lifeboat.

Exploration

- Did anyone not share any of the information on their card?

- If not, why not in terms of status?

- Who would normally have high status?

- Who would normally have low status?

- Did people who would normally have high status fare better or worse?

- Did people who would normally have low status fare better or worse?

- Who had the highest status and why?

- What was most important in this situation: status, skills or ability to argue your point?

- How is this like real life?

Comments

This exercise demonstrates how status can easily shift depending on the context. Previous experiences of running this exercise have resulted in interesting discussions around the importance of saving parents, young people, those whom the group consider to have high status and those who have practical skills useful in a survival situation. It is often those who are more articulate at getting their point across who end up being saved, regardless of their characteristics. The facilitator may want to prompt discussion by commenting that the experience of the sinking ship may cause some characters to re-evaluate and change their lives. Therefore it might be interesting for participants to reflect on how the situation might affect their character's future.

Sinking Ships character cards

Doctor **Male, 59. Married with three children, seven grandchildren. Hobbies include golf and travel.**	**Rapper** **Female, 23. Single, no children. Has had two number one singles.**
Shop assistant **Female, 33. Single with two children. Favourite music is R&B.**	**Youth worker** **Male, 28. Married with one child. Has several swimming medals.**
Survival expert **Male, 42. Married with no children. Wants to emigrate to Australia.**	**Ship's captain** **Female, 38. Single, no children. Interested in astronomy.**
Judge **Male, 72. Widower with four children, 13 grandchildren. Likes wine tasting.**	**MP** **Male, 54. Lives with partner, no children. Campaigns for equal rights.**
Artist **Female, 58. Single, no children. Campaigns against cruelty to animals.**	**Chef** **Male, 41. Single, no children. Speciality is fish.**
Unemployed **Male, 18. Single, no children. Enjoys spending time with friends.**	**Boxer** **Male, 28. Single, three children. Likes to party.**
Police officer **Male, 26. Single, no children. Does voluntary work for local community.**	

3.4 Status And Power

Time: 20 min

Explanation

A role-play exercise looking at status and power.

Intention

To gain insight into the impact that status and power have on the roles we play and how we play them.

Equipment

Scenario cards (see p.88).

Instructions

1. The facilitator divides the group into pairs. Each pair is given a set of scenario cards. One is to play character A and the other character B.

2. Each pair is asked to spend five minutes rehearsing their scenes.

3. The facilitator brings the big group back together and the scenes are shown back. After each scene the facilitator asks participants who they thought had the most status and who they thought had the most power.

Exploration

- How easy/difficult was it to stay in character?

- When and how do people use their status?

- When and how do people use their power?

- Is power always connected with a role/position in society?

- How is status different from power?

- Can status give you power?

Comments

This exercise aims to explore the complicated relationship between status and power. Status relates to positioning within a social group and often power accompanies status. This is because those with high status may have a wider range of choices available to them and choices can give power. Everybody, regardless of their status, has choices available to them. Thus it is still possible to be powerful when you have low status. For example, when Nelson Mandela was initially imprisoned, as a prisoner he had low status. However, because of the dignity with which he conducted himself as a prisoner, that is, speaking courteously to the guards and showing an interest in them as human beings, he became respected by them and his status with them began to shift. Mandela used the limited power he had in that situation to choose to serve the sentence he was given in a certain way. In this particular instance Mandela's choices shifted his status from low to high. Status does not always shift through the effective use of power, but it is important to remember that however limited our choices appear to be we always have a choice in how we deal with any situation. The scenarios on the cards are set up so that the person with seemingly low status can increase their power by making effective choices.

Status and Power scenario cards

Character A You are a gang leader. You borrowed an iPod from another member of the gang and you have lost it. **Character B** You are a gang member. You lent your iPod to the gang leader and they have lost it.	**Character A** You are the manager of a high-class clothes shop. A customer is returning a faulty item. You know it is faulty. The customer does not have their receipt. **Character B** You have bought an item of clothing from a high-class shop. You washed it according to the instructions and it has shrunk. You have lost your receipt.
Character A You have been in an accident with a prominent football player; it is the footballer's fault the accident happened. **Character B** You are a prominent football player. You have been in an accident with someone and it was your fault.	**Character A** You have been arrested for a crime you did not commit. **Character B** You are a police officer under pressure to find the person who has committed a crime. You believe that the person you have arrested is guilty of that crime.
Character A You are at an interview for a job you really want. You feel the person interviewing you is being discriminatory. **Character B** You are interviewing a candidate for a job. You feel the person is too young for the job.	**Character A** Your friend's parent has made a special meal for you to celebrate your birthday. You do not like what they have cooked. **Character B** Your child's friend has come over for a birthday meal that you have spent a long time preparing.

3.5 Taking A Risk

Time: 20 min

Explanation

A small groupwork exercise exploring some of the risks people might take in order to gain status.

Intention

To gain insight into the costs and gains of risk-taking behaviour.

Instructions

1. The facilitator asks the participants to think about some of the risks people might take in order to gain status, e.g. fighting, joyriding.

2. In groups of four, participants will create a tableau showing a gang doing something that other people may think is risky.

3. Each group in turn shows back their picture and gives an explanation of what the gang is doing and why.

4. The participants watching rate the level of risk from 1 to 5, 1 being the lowest risk level.

Exploration

- How are risk taking and status linked?

- What happens to people who don't have status?

- What can be the gains of taking risks to increase status?

- What can be the costs?

Comments

Risky behaviour mainly impacts on status if others witness it. A gang may take a risk as it sends a message about its status to members of the rival gang. Getting the better of someone with high status can increase the status of the challenger. The status attached to taking an illegal risk, e.g. graffiti, is different from the status attached to taking a legal risk, e.g. bungy jumping, because there is a different type of kudos associated with the risk. When this groupwork programme is run in conjunction with an activity programme, this exercise provides an opportunity to explore how the risks (or lack of risks) taken by participants impact on their status. It may be interesting to explore with a group the other kinds of risks they may take. For example, some of the work they are doing as part of the groupwork programme may result in them feeling vulnerable or uncomfortable at times as they are asked and encouraged to share personal information about themselves with others. The costs and benefits of taking this kind of risk may not have an immediate impact on increasing their status. It may, however, result in them making more positive choices in their lives which could mean that eventually their status is based on firmer foundations.

3.6 Second Guessing

Time: 15 min

Explanation

A whole group warm-up exercise.

Intention

To begin thinking about the assumptions we make about people.

Instructions

1.   The two facilitators agree on four facts about themselves that are not particularly obvious, e.g. I was born in Africa, I have a degree in history.

2.   The facilitators write these eight statements on the flip chart and the participants guess which one is true about which facilitator.

Exploration

- What do we base our ideas about other people on?

- Why do we do this?

- How can making assumptions help us?

- How can making assumptions limit us?

Comments

This exercise is most effective if the facts that the facilitators agree on are seemingly more likely to be true about the other person. For instance, if there is a male and a female facilitator and the female is a DJ it is less likely that the group will guess this correctly. Our assumptions about people are often based on stereotypes and past experiences. Used well this exercise can really shake a group's certainty around the habitual assumptions that they make about others. It can then become a reference point for other situations where individuals or the group make snap judgements about others.

3.7 Myths

Time: 55 min

Explanation

A large group discussion using tableau to explore social myths.

Intention

To explore where myths come from and the impact they have.

Instructions

1. The facilitator starts by asking participants 'What is a myth?' The facilitator inputs that there is some fact and some story in a myth and the idea tends to get passed on to others.

2. The facilitator draws the following diagram on a piece of flip-chart paper. He or she continues by asking the following sequence of questions and writing the answers to each question in a separate circle:

What are some of the myths that some people hold about your
group/gang? (e.g. You're all violent thugs/criminals)

How can they work
against you?

Where do myths about
your group come from?

What are the myths that
you play up to? Why?

How does each myth
affect you? Your life?

How do they affect what your family say/feel about the group
you hang around with?

3.   The facilitator then divides participants into two groups. Group A makes a tableau of a myth about their group and group B has to guess it. They then swap over.

Exploration

- What have you done to gain a myth?

- Are you happy with the myths people hold about you?

- What are the negative things people say about you and your group?

- How do you feel when you are called this?

- How do you react?

- What is the consequence?

- Does this reinforce what people think about you?

- How does this become a self-fulfilling prophecy?

- Is there anything you can do to change the myth about you?

- How are myth and reputation linked?

Comments

This exercise begins to explore the issue of reputation. Myth and reputation are linked as they both tend to involve a mixture of fact and fiction. When the myths about a group are unpicked it can be seen that group members play a part in influencing some of the stories people hold about them. Some myths will be deliberately encouraged by the group's behaviour as it increases their status. Myths can become self-fulfilling prophecies as playing up to a myth will serve to reinforce it. Myths are cyclical and it is likely that there may be a lot that is common in the answers to the first and last questions.

3.8 Jailbreak

Time: 15 min

Explanation

An active group game.

Intention

To energise and warm up participants. To consider where participants get caught up in patterns of behaviour.

Instructions

1. The participants begin by sitting in a circle.

2. The facilitator counts off the participants, numbering them one, two, one, two, all round the circle. They ask the number twos to remove their chairs from the circle and to stand behind the chairs of the number ones. An odd number is needed for this game so the second facilitator should only join in if needed.

3. The facilitator stands behind an empty chair. They explain that the game is called Jailbreak and the people standing behind the chairs are jailers. Their job is to keep the people sitting down in their jail (the prisoners). Jailers must stand at arm's length behind their prisoners. The role of the prisoners is to escape from their jail.

4. The facilitator has an empty jail at the start of the game and their goal is to get someone in it. They do this by winking at someone who is sitting down.

5. The prisoner who is winked at must try to escape from their jail without being touched by their jailer. If the prisoner escapes, they go and sit in the jailer's chair. If the jailer touches them, they must remain in their jail and the facilitator must wink at another prisoner.

6. When a new jail becomes vacant, that jailer becomes the winker.

7. After five minutes, ask the prisoners and jailers to swap roles.

Exploration

- How did you find that game?

- When you were a jailer, what strategies did you use to keep people in your jail?

- When you were a jailer, what strategies did you use to get people in your jail?

- How did it feel when you couldn't get out of your jail?

- What strategies did you try?

- Who got out of jail?

- Where did you go?

- How is this like life?

Comments

This game helps participants to think about their habitual patterns of behaviour. When prisoners escape from their jail they are simply entering another similar jail. This is often the way with conflict until techniques are developed which create more choice. Our habitual responses to conflict keep us locked in a cycle of behaviour that may not get us where we want to go. In order to get where we want to be, new responses to conflict need to be learned.

3.9 I've Got The Power

Time: 20 min

Explanation

An individual exercise in which participants fill in a power inventory.

Intention

To gain insight into the different areas where we hold power.

Equipment

Photocopies of the Power Inventory (p.98).

Instructions

1. The facilitator hands a Power Inventory to all participants.

2. Each participant fills in the boxes with a number from 1 to 5, with 1 representing that they feel they have little power in this situation and 5 representing that they feel they have a lot of power over the situation.

3. Once all participants have filled in their inventories they share them with a partner.

4. The facilitator can then input that there are different types of power. 'Positional' power is based on the status of the individual, e.g. boss and employee. 'Personal' power is based on personality. 'Physical' power is based on size.

Exploration

- What contributes to us feeling powerless in different situations?

- What makes us feel powerful?

- How can we become more powerful?

Comments

Positional, personal and physical powers are not mutually exclusive. Some people may hold all three whilst others may hold none at all. In a conflict situation it may be that those involved hold different types of power, e.g. a small-framed police officer in conflict with a large-framed young person. In these instances the different types of power will be asserted to varying degrees. Groups that are comfortable in their relationship with each other may be willing to explore who in their group holds which type of power and how these powers can be used effectively. It is interesting to explore with the gang their own unique power dynamic. In some gangs the leaders may be focused on studying and in others the leaders may regularly get into physical conflicts. The attributes of the gang leader usually have a trickle-down effect and influence the character of the gang as a whole.

Power Inventory: How powerful do you feel?

1 = I feel powerless   5 = I feel powerful

At home?	
In the centre of town alone?	
In the centre of town with friends?	
In your bedroom?	
In a police station	
In a foreign country?	
With your friends?	
Alone in a part of town you don't know?	
With friends in a part of town you don't know?	
On a football pitch/netball court?	
In your community?	
At school/college?	
In a car?	
At a job interview?	
In society as a whole?	
In a conflict?	

3.10 The Powerful And The Powerless

Time: 35 min

Explanation

A physical groupwork exercise where participants explore how they perceive themselves.

Intention

To express how you see yourself in relation to power.

Instructions

1. The facilitators get two chairs and place them at opposite ends of the room. They put a piece of paper on one chair reading 'powerful' and a piece on the other reading 'powerless'.

2. The participants are told that there is a line between the two chairs. If you stand by one chair then you see yourself as being powerful. If you stand by the other chair you see yourself as being powerless. Participants can stand anywhere they want along the line, e.g. if they feel fairly powerful they may stand two-thirds of the way along the line.

3. The facilitator asks: 'How powerful do you see yourself as a…'

   • young man or young woman?

   • member of your ethnic group?

   • young person?

   • student/person looking for a job?

   • person able to achieve your ambitions?

   • member of your friendship group?

   • member of your family?

   • physically big/small person?

4. At each question the facilitator can check in with participants for an explanation of why they have put themselves in a particular place. If a participant hears something that makes them want to move they can do so.

Exploration

• How do you see yourself?

• Where are you the most powerful?

• Where are you the least powerful?

- Did anyone find themselves in a position they did not like?

- Was anyone surprised about where they were on the line?

- Is there a difference between how you see yourself and how society sees you?

- How do other members of your group see you?

- Does the group/gang see things about you that other people don't?

- Would you like the group/gang to see you differently?

Comments

This exercise helps to highlight that how we perceive ourselves in terms of our own power may be very different from how others see us in relation to power. When running this exercise with a gang with both male and female members it was interesting that the young men felt the young women were more powerful because they were able to pick who they had a relationship with. The young women felt the young men were more powerful as they were perceived as a physical threat to their rival gang.

3.11 Push Me If You Can

Time: 15 min

Explanation

An active group game.

Intention

To energise participants and explore different sources of power.

Instructions

1. The facilitator asks the participants to find a partner.

2. The pairs stand toe to toe with the palms of their hands touching.

3. Each participant's aim is to get their partner to take one step backwards. They can only do this by pushing their hands. Participants can move their hands as much as they like.

4. After two minutes the pairs swap partners. This is done until participants have swapped partners three times.

Exploration

*   What was it like facing a person who was much stronger than you?

*   Did anyone who thought they were much stronger than the person facing them still end up taking one step backwards?

*   What's it like to be confident/unconfident in your physical power?

*   How much does your physical power influence your status in the gang?

*   What role does your physical power play in this exercise?

*   What other types of power were needed to get your partner to step backwards?

*   What are the ways of being powerful without using physical power?

Comments

On the surface this exercise seems to be about physical power. In practice it becomes apparent that it is possible for someone very small to push someone much larger backwards. This is because when participants are standing toe to toe it is balance rather than physical force that is important. This exercise highlights the different types of power available to us. The use of strategies such as going to the left when the other person is going to the right results in the use of intellectual power to overcome a hurdle.

3.12 Boxing Ring

Time: 60 min

Explanation

A structured role-play involving skill development and coaching support.

Intention

To practise difficult situations and explore the power balance in these situations.

Instructions

1. The facilitator asks for two volunteers. One will take on the role of a young person being stopped by a police officer (the challenger) and the other will take on the role of the policeman/woman (the opponent).

2. Four more volunteers take on the role of coaches: two for the young person and two for the officer.

3. The other participants act as observers.

4. The challenger must have a clear goal, e.g. they are late for an interview and want the police officer to hurry up. In order to achieve this goal, the challenger must communicate their position effectively.

5. The opponent also has a goal, e.g. they want to talk to the young person about a street robbery that has recently taken place. They have no evidence to take the challenger to the station so they are going to try and provoke them into an angry reaction. The opponent should be asked to play their role sensitively as the overall aim of the exercise is to support the participant playing the challenger to practise doing something different in difficult situations.

6. The challenger and the opponent both have a few minutes to get into character and devise their stories with the help of their coaches.

7. The facilitator explains that they will be playing the role of referee. A boxing ring is marked out with chairs. The participants playing the young person and policeman/woman sit facing each other. Slightly behind them sit their two coaches.

8. The referee takes control of the timing of the round. They also decide the starting point, e.g. the police officer has just stopped the young person. They will decide when each round begins and ends and notify the participants by sounding the bell. They can also call 'time out' if either participant is struggling.

9. The role of the coaches is to support the challenger and opponent in their goals. At the end of the rounds and during 'time out' the coaches will feed

back what they are doing well and what is not working. They can also suggest strategies and let the role-player know if they are being realistic. They cannot comment during the rounds.

10. The observers will feed back at the end of the fight. Their role is to comment on how appropriate the coaching was. Did the role-player get enough/too much support? What strategies did the role-players use that worked?

Exploration

- Who has positional/personal power in these situations?

- How did the power balance affect communication?

- What made communication more easy/difficult?

- What changes if the person you are communicating with is your friend/enemy?

- What support worked/didn't work in this exercise?

- What was it like giving support to others?

- What was it like receiving support from others?

- Did anyone try any new strategies?

- How did they work?

Once this exercise has been completed the facilitator can also ask the group to come up with their own challenges or use these possible scenarios:

- Two young people, one wants the other to back them up in a fight whilst the other doesn't want to get involved.

- A young person is having a conversation with their parent as the parent does not want them to go to a party with their friends.

Comments

This exercise provides the possibility of discovering new strategies for habitual responses to conflict and new ways of perceiving difficulties in situations that participants are entrenched in and finding hard to change. The facilitator may need to support the coaches in coaching the opponent and challenger effectively. The coaches' feedback should explore whether or not the opponent or challenger is communicating their position in a way that is most likely to get them heard, e.g. using non-aggressive language, responding to facts and not interpretation; whether or not they are presenting a realistic challenge and how the dialogue can move forward. If the challenger is not getting closer to their goal the facilitator may ask the opponent to tone down their role-playing or support the challenger by giving them some ideas about using a different approach. Groups can sometimes get very excited in this exercise and it is important to maintain the balance of fun and effective learning. De-roling (see p.17) is a useful tool for bringing participants back from the exercise.

Chapter 4

Enemies and Revenge

> When it comes to attacking people we attack back. Back in the 1980s if people got attacked they would just ignore them. Now if someone gets attacked people join in and help them by fighting back, not ignoring it.
>
> We always fight in the summer when everyone is fighting and they are jealous. People remember faces from the past and want conflict again.
>
> We do fight with black people, 'cos we see them as a different race. When certain groups of black boys get together they just call us 'Somalian'. The Somalian boy gets angry and just runs into them.
>
> *Participants from Leap's action research project*

Most gangs have an enemy gang. Conflict between gangs is often rooted in the conflict between individuals. Over time the individuals who are locked in conflict involve those people who are close to them. Resolving the conflict between these groups may hinge on the successful resolution of the conflict between the original adversaries.

Most children learn to have enemies from an early age. These enemies may be members of a particular ethnic group, religion, occupation or any stranger or particular person. Some gang conflicts have a history older than many of those involved in the conflict. The children who are born into the gang conflict may not know the history behind it but they do know that there is an expectation regarding how they should behave towards the enemy.

Over the past 50 years much of the gang conflict in the UK has occurred between different racial groups. There have been areas that were no-go for people of certain ethnicities. These days race may be a factor in gang conflict but it is not necessarily the defining factor. Some areas experience fighting in which the rival gangs are from different ethnic backgrounds. In others the gangs are multi-ethnic and elsewhere fighting between gangs of the same ethnic group can be found.

Young people who are involved in fighting within their own ethnic group are usually in conflict with young people of the same social background, who wear the same clothes, listen to the same music, are the same age, have the same hopes and fears and even go to the same schools. Carl Jung's work shows that what we find unacceptable in ourselves we attribute to our enemy and then dissociate from ourselves (Jung 1981). From this viewpoint gang fighting and the creation of enemies can be seen as a response to young people's negative self-image.

Once someone becomes your enemy, certain behaviours that might usually be unacceptable are now considered legitimate. When an incident takes place between rival gangs there is usually a 'winner' and a 'loser'. One of the groups is often left feeling the need to take revenge. There is pressure on the group to get revenge otherwise they might be considered weak and therefore a target. The gang considers getting revenge to be getting even. The type of revenge taken relates to the incident that it is in response to. This creates a vicious cycle of revenge.

Key questions

This chapter encourages participants to ask themselves:

- Who are my enemies?

- Who would I be without my enemies?

Aims

- To examine what is meant by the word 'enemy'.

- To explore how 'enemies' are created.

- To look at the costs and gains of getting revenge.

- To understand what is being created in a culture of revenge.

Enemies and Revenge Day Plan

Day Intro	10.00	5 min
Gathering – Something someone has done recently that you appreciate	10.05	10 min
Game – Bombs And Shields	10.15	15 min
Enemy Thinking	10.30	30 min
Enemies And Power	11.00	15 min
BREAK	11.15	20 min
Outsiders	11.35	15 min
My Enemy	11.50	25 min
Underlying Anger	12.15	45 min
LUNCH	1.00	60 min
Gathering – Share an example of a time you have taken revenge	2.00	10 min
Game – Grandma's Keys	2.10	15 min
Whose Side Are You On?	2.25	30 min
Who's Affected?	2.55	30 min
BREAK	3.25	20 min
Game – Paranoia	3.45	15 min
The Gamble Of Revenge	4.00	55 min
Close	4.55	5 min

4.1 Bombs And Shields

Time: 15 min

Explanation

An active whole group game.

Intention

To begin thinking about who or what acts as a 'bomb' or a 'shield' in our lives.

Instructions

1. Each participant is asked to choose one other person in the group, but not to tell that person they have been chosen.

2. The facilitator explains to the participants that the person they have chosen is their 'bomb' and they must keep as far away as possible from that person.

3. The facilitator calls 'start' and the group moves round the room for a minute.

4. The participants are then asked to pick another person in the room without saying who it is. This person is their 'shield' and they must keep this person between themselves and their 'bomb'.

5. The facilitator starts this part of the exercise and allows it to continue for a few minutes.

6. The facilitator calls 'stop'. If some of the group continue moving until they are in a safe space the facilitator should either let the group start again, ensuring they stop dead, or keep an eye out and ask specific people to move back to the positions they were in before 'stop' was called.

7. The facilitator should go round the group finding out who is safe by asking who participants' 'bombs' are and who their 'shields' are and seeing if their 'shield' is positioned between them and their 'bomb'.

Exploration

- What did it feel like avoiding your 'bomb' in the first part?

- Who had control?

- Who or what are 'bombs' in your life?

- What was it like trying to stay behind your 'shield'?

- Who had control?

- Who or what are 'shields' in your life?

- Can your 'bombs' and 'shields' ever be the same person/thing?

- In real life, who are the 'bombs' in this group?

- What do they do to make themselves 'bombs'?

- In real life, who are the 'shields' in this group?

- What do they do to make themselves 'shields'?

Comments

This exercise helps participants to think about the different effects that people in their lives can have on them. 'Shields' can protect you, e.g. friends; 'bombs' can cause danger, e.g. a rival gang. In many cases 'bombs' and 'shields' are the same person or thing, e.g. family, a friend who when you are around often gets drawn into trouble. In this exercise the 'bombs' and 'shields' whom the participants chose had the power to make them move. In real life, our 'bombs' and 'shields' can also determine our actions if we react to them without thinking or making a clear and conscious choice to respond differently.

4.2 Enemy Thinking

Time: 30 min

Explanation

A wordstorm to gather ideas and perceptions of what 'enemy' means to the group, moving into paired work and whole group discussion to explore our relationship to our enemies.

Intention

To establish a starting point for work on enemies and to gain insight into the different types of enemy.

Instructions

1. To lead into this exercise the facilitator asks the participants:

    - Which groups of people don't you like?

    - Which groups of people do you hate?

    - Which groups of people are your enemies?

2. The facilitator then asks the participants to wordstorm the concept of enemy by asking:

    - What does the word 'enemy' mean to you?

    - Who were you taught to see as your enemy? What groups were you taught to see as your enemy? By whom?

    - What feelings do you associate with the word enemy?

    - What facts do you associate with the word enemy?

3. The facilitator asks the participants to discuss:

    - How do you make enemies?

    - What do people have to do to become your enemy?

    - Are your enemies the same as your parent's enemies?

    - Have your enemies changed in your lifetime?

    - Do you expect your enemies to stay the same throughout your lifetime?

4. In pairs, the participants talk about their experiences with different types of enemy.

5. The facilitator brings the participants back together and asks them to share some of their experiences.

Exploration

- What's the difference between the feelings of dislike and hate?

- Are some enemies 'worse' than other enemies?

- Can our enemies become our allies?

- What do we gain/lose by having enemies?

- What happens to groups when their enemy is removed or changes?

Comments

For some gangs, and in particular some gang leaders, having enemies gives a sense of power, identity and self-esteem. This issue should be explored very carefully when bringing rival gangs together as some members may feel they have more to lose than to gain through a peaceful reconciliation. In these situations alternative sources of power, identity and self-esteem need to be looked at with the groups.

4.3 Enemies And Power

Time: 15 min

Explanation

An individual tableau exercise exploring the concept of 'enemy'.

Intention

To explore our perception of enemies.

Instructions

1.   The participants are asked to stand up in a circle. Everyone turns around so they are facing outside the circle. The participants are given 30 seconds to think about what their frozen image of the word 'enemy' would look like. On the count of three everyone turns in and displays their image.

2.   One by one the facilitator focuses on each participant's image. Participants should be asked to notice the physical characteristics of the different stances, e.g. do they lean forwards or backwards? The facilitator will ask the young person to explain why they have taken a particular form. The participants are encouraged to see any links between different people's statues.

Exploration

- What did some of the statues have in common?

- What were some of the differences?

- Were there any surprises?

- Do we see our statues as having power?

- Do we see them as being powerful?

- Do we see them as having more or less power than us?

Comments

In this exercise it can be seen that there are common ways that we see our enemies even though they are our enemies for different reasons. It is likely that many of the frozen images will show people standing tall, with fists clenched or arms raised and leaning forward. This is because we typically view our enemies as aggressive, power hungry and intent on winning.

4.4 Outsiders

Time: 15 min

Explanation

A group exercise exploring the effects of being outside the main group.

Intention

To look at how we react to rejection and how it feels to be part of a group.

Instructions

1. Ask a volunteer to leave the room. The remainder of the participants divide themselves into groups according to some agreed criteria, e.g. hairstyle, eye colour, accent.

2. The outsider is called and guesses which group they belong to. They must state why they believe that is their group. If the reason is wrong they may not join, even when they have picked the correct group.

3. Let as many volunteers have a go as time allows.

Exploration

- How do we behave when we belong to a group?

- Is it easy to reject outsiders?

- Is it enjoyable?

- Do we empathise with the outsider or do we enjoy the power?

- How does it feel to be part of a large group?

- How does it feel to be excluded?

- What are the situations in participants' lives where they have felt excluded/not belonged?

- How does it feel to be outside the main group?

- Do you exclude people from your group?

- If yes, why?

Comments

It is common when running this exercise for participants to take particular pleasure in excluding the person outside the room. Being part of a majority can lead to people feeling safe, comfortable, complacent and powerful in relation to outsiders. They may also want to protect that group or keep other people out in order to preserve the identity of the group and those feelings of safety, comfort and power. In turn, being isolated can lead to feelings of insecurity, danger and loneliness. As well as being physically excluded there are many other ways that people can be excluded. The facilitator might want to discuss some of these with the group, e.g. being excluded from certain bits of information/knowledge, being excluded because of dyslexia. Groups can be asked to reflect on how it might feel for people in their area/school who are not part of their group.

4.5 My Enemy

Time: 25 min

Explanation

A paired tableau exercise looking at personal enemies and rival gang members.

Intention

To examine our enemies and introduce the concept of the shadow enemy.

Instructions

1. Put participants into pairs and ask them to choose A and B. Next ask A to sculpt B into a picture of a member of their rival gang. For example, A sculpts B into a person holding a knife.

2. B then responds by sculpting A into a statue that represents how the statue B might see A. For example, B might sculpt A as someone running away.

3. Ask each group to show back their tableau to the larger group and ask A and B how they feel as the statues. Ask each person to think as their statue and finish the sentence 'You are my enemy because...'

4. If there is time, ask A and B to swap round.

Exploration

- Are there any common characteristics between A and B?
- How did it feel for A to be sculpted by B?
- What is the root of their hatred?
- What threatens them? What do we and our enemies have in common?
- What fears do we share?
- What threats do we represent to each other?
- What would need to happen for you to work with your enemy?

Comments

This exercise explores the similarities between participants and their enemies. Often the characteristics that are disliked about the enemy are also true for the self, e.g. unwilling to back down in an argument, loud and boisterous. Sometimes it is the things that we don't like about ourselves that we project onto our enemies. One pair we worked with in Scotland chose the police as their enemy. This pair acknowledged that the things they didn't like about the police – looking for trouble, always supporting each other and operating in large groups – were likely to be the same things that the police didn't like about their gang.

✓

4.6 Underlying Anger

Time: 45 min

Explanation

A written exercise which explores what underlies anger.

Intention

To encourage participants to consider what lies behind an instance of personal anger.

Equipment

The facilitator should prepare a piece of flip-chart paper by drawing a copy of the diagram below and folding the paper so each of the four levels can be revealed one by one. Enough photocopies of the diagram should be made ready.

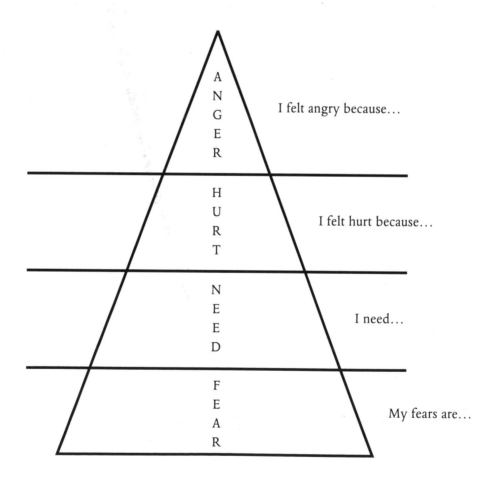

Instructions

1. The facilitator begins by asking the participants what they know about icebergs until they have established that the majority of an iceberg is hidden. The facilitator then inputs that when we see an expression of anger we only see what is visible, e.g. shouting. We do not see what is underneath the anger.

2. The facilitator gives an example of a situation that has made them angry, e.g. 'I shouted at my colleague when they turned up late.' The facilitator inputs the distinction between the cause of the anger (colleague being late) and the expression of the anger (shouting).

3. The facilitator then explains that a layer of hurt often underlies anger, e.g. 'I felt hurt because I had rushed to make sure I wasn't late.'

4. The reason for the hurt is often an unmet need, e.g. 'I need to have my time recognised/valued.' The facilitator can input that needs can be both emotional (as above) or practical, e.g. 'I need my colleague to phone me if they are running late.'

5. Alongside the need are often fears, e.g. 'I fear that my colleague does not have a professional approach and that will affect me negatively and lose me work.' The facilitator can input that fears can be both rational (as above) or irrational, e.g. 'I fear that my colleague is deliberately being late to annoy me.'

6. The facilitator then asks participants to fill in their own iceberg.

7. Once they have finished participants share their four sentences with a partner. If anyone has had difficulty identifying the layers, their partner can help them. If there is time, volunteers can share back to the whole group.

Exploration

- What is the value of understanding anger?

- Do you think people who are viewing the anger expressed understand what the fear at the bottom is?

- How can understanding the root of our anger help us in life?

Comments

This exercise is also effective when looking at the group's underlying anger. The group can be asked to think of a situation where they were angry as a whole and work through the different layers of the iceberg. The participants will have different hurts, needs and fears and these can all be filled in on a collective diagram. For instance, some participants may climb onto their friend's iceberg when their friend is angry with someone. It is also worth pointing out that if participants see somebody else getting angry they could try to view that expression of anger as an expression of something deeper and this might change their response to that person.

4.7 Grandma's Keys

Time: 15 min

Explanation

An active group game.

Intention

To explore feelings around risk taking and working cooperatively. To energise.

Instructions

1. Ask a volunteer to stand at one end of the room facing the wall. This person will be Grandma. Behind them place a large set of jangly keys on the ground.

2. The rest of the participants start at the other end of the room. They attempt to creep up behind Grandma and collect the keys. At any point Grandma can turn round. When this happens everyone must stop. If Grandma sees anyone move she calls out and they have to go back to the beginning.

3. Once someone has successfully collected the keys they become Grandma.

4. After a few different people have had a chance to be Grandma a new dimension can be introduced. The participants are told that in order to win they must collect the keys and bring them back to the start line. Once the keys have been collected, they must pass through the hands of three participants before crossing the start line.

5. Once the keys have been collected, any time Grandma turns round she can guess who has the keys. If she guesses correctly all the participants have to go back to the beginning. If not the game continues.

Exploration

*   Which version of the game did you prefer?

*   How did it feel to be sent back?

*   How did it feel to be Grandma?

*   How did it feel when you had the keys?

*   Did the group decide on a strategy to get the keys?

*   How was that strategy agreed?

- Did anyone take any risks?

- How is this game like real life?

Comments

Participants attempting to get the keys at the group stage have talked of feelings of camaraderie, fun and cunning. It usually takes a group a few attempts to get the keys before they devise a strategy. Strategies used to get the keys include having everyone bend down around the keys and having everyone hold their hands behind their backs. In previous experiences of running this game participants being Grandma have expressed a feeling of being ganged up on in the group stage. The game has been likened to trying to get away from the police with gang members deliberately presenting a confusing front in the hope that they will avoid detection.

4.8 Whose Side Are You On?

Time: 30 min

Explanation

An active whole group exercise to explore the different roles we take in conflict.

Intention

To gain insight into why we take the roles we do in conflict and what impact this has on the conflict.

Preparation

In this exercise the facilitators will role-play an argument. This is agreed on and practised prior to the exercise. For example, one facilitator might accuse the other of barging them. The argument gradually escalates until it reaches boiling point. The facilitators should think carefully about what they might say to escalate the argument, e.g. threatening behaviour, insulting the other person's family, as the participants are going to be asked to change sides according to who they feel is being wronged.

Instructions

1. Explain to the participants that they are going to see a staged argument and that they should decide whose side to be on according to who they feel is being wronged. The participants can change sides throughout the argument.
2. The facilitator asks everyone to stand and begins the action.
3. Each time the argument escalates a degree the facilitator stops the action and asks the participants to move to whose side they are on.
4. The exercise continues until the argument reaches boiling point.

Exploration

- How did you decide whose side to take?
- Who did you really want to go with?
- Who switched sides?
- What made you switch sides?
- How easy is it to switch sides in real life?
- What would a friend have to do for you to not offer them support/back-up in a conflict?
- When did you start thinking about yourself in the conflict?

- What happens when people take sides?

- What role did the onlookers have in the conflict?

- What's not happening in this situation?

- How can you get the whole story?

Comments

This exercise highlights the impact of taking sides and observing conflict. Even as by-standers participants are choosing to take a role that will impact on the conflict. It is more difficult for those arguing to back down when there are onlookers stirring up the action. Often when running this exercise the onlookers will not follow the instruction to change sides according to who is being wronged. They will move according to who they think is putting up the best argument. Sometimes something will be said that the onlookers find unacceptable, e.g. sexual insults directed at one of the role-player's mothers, and participants will not move sides regardless of what is said following this. In one experience of running this exercise one of the participants took a mediating position between the two people arguing. During the exploration he commented that in real life he would find this a very difficult position to take because he feels a pressure to support his friends, even if he thinks they are in the wrong.

4.9 Who's Affected?

Time: 30 min

Explanation

A group exercise looking at a real or an imaginary group conflict.

Intention

To explore the impact of a gang conflict on various different groups.

Instructions

1. Four pieces of flip-chart paper are stuck together and a large circle is drawn in the middle. The paper is then put on the floor. The participants are told that this represents a fight between two gangs in which a gang member seriously hurts someone in the other gang. The incident can be real or imaginary (see p.17 for more discussion of this).

2. The participants are then asked to spend three minutes with the person next to them thinking about who is affected by the incident, e.g. friends, family, community, police.

3. The participants are brought back together and they share their discussion. The names of the different groups affected are written on strips of paper. The participants are asked to place the strips on the circle: the people who are most affected are nearest the centre of the circle, those least affected are further away and placed around the circle.

4. Participants are then asked to act as representatives of each of the groups. They stand on the strip and imagine how those people might have been affected. The facilitator taps different participants and they speak about how they were affected by the situation.

Exploration

- Who is affected and how?
- Who has a choice about being involved?
- Whose well-being goes up?
- Whose well-being goes down?
- Whose status/reputation increases?
- Whose status/reputation decreases?
- How does the power balance shift?

- What might happen next?

- How might this affect people?

- Who has the power to do something different?

- Who has the power to start/stop the conflict?

Comments

The key to this exercise is in exploring who has the power to stop/start the conflict. One group we worked with felt that only they had the power to stop the conflict. Whilst it is true that only they are responsible for their actions, the facilitator might explore with participants whether anyone else has the power to affect the conflict, e.g. a group of concerned parents on an estate, parents from rival gangs getting together. Bystanders often have the power to make an impact. Sometimes by just standing and witnessing they can affect the outcome of a conflict. We all have some power to support others in de-escalating conflict according to our relationship to the protagonists, the context in which the conflict is happening, our own ability to deal with conflict and our own sense of personal safety.

4.10 Paranoia

Time: 15 min

Explanation

A whole group exercise looking at concentration and cooperation (adapted from the *Geese Theatre Handbook* [Baim, Brookes and Mountford 2002; reprinted in 2006], with kind permission of the Geese Theatre Company and Waterside Press, www.watersidepress.co.uk).

Intention

To explore the impact of waiting for something to happen.

Equipment

Small pieces of paper with a different number for all but one of the participants, e.g. if there are 15 participants the slips are numbered 1–14.

Instructions

1. The participants stand in a circle with a volunteer in the middle. The rest of the participants take a numbered slip. They do not let anyone know their number.

2. The volunteer calls out two numbers. The aim is for the two participants with these numbered slips to change places before the person in the middle takes one of their places. The two participants who have these numbers secretly make contact with each other to arrange the switch, e.g. by winking.

3. If the person in the middle does not manage to take one of the places on the outside of the circle they continue to call out numbers until they are successful.

4. Once the person in the middle has made it to the outside the numbered slips are put in a pile and redistributed.

5. The facilitator chooses for the game to finish when they feel everyone has had a go.

Exploration

- What was it like being in the middle?

- What was it like when your number was called and you were looking for the other person?

- How did you make contact and agree to change places?

- Did you prefer being on the outside or in the middle?

- Why?

- What connections are there between this exercise and life outside this group?

- What's it like having to avoid detection?

- What's it like waiting for something to happen that is out of your control?

Comments

This game introduces the concept of waiting for something to happen that is out of our control. It is likely that participants on the outside of the circle will try to trick the person in the middle into believing that they have the number that has been called. This creates a sense of danger and anticipation that can be related to the feelings experienced after an incident where one gang is attacked by their rivals. In these instances the attacking gang are left having to wait to see what and when revenge will be taken.

4.11 The Gamble Of Revenge

Time: 55 min

Explanation

A paired exercise in which participants undertake different types of revenge on each other.

Intention

To explore what is created in the culture of revenge.

Equipment

Several sets of dice, scenario cards (see p.128).

Instructions

1. Ask the participants to wordstorm different types of revenge. Encourage them to think of both minor and major forms of revenge.

2. Next ask the group to think about some of the feelings and needs that go with revenge.

3. Decide on six examples of revenge that grade from minor to major, for example:

   - dirty look

   - cussing

   - fighting

   - stealing property

   - snitching

   - extreme violence.

4. Divide the participants into pairs and give each pair a set of scenario cards and two dice.

5. Player one is the protagonist. They pick a scenario card and read it out loud.

6. Player one then rolls the dice. The number the dice lands on relates to the type of revenge they must take (see instruction 3). They create a tableau image of the revenge they carry out.

7. Player two then rolls the dice. The number the dice lands on relates to the level of revenge they will take on player one.

8. Bring the pairs back together to form one large group. Ask each pair to show their tableau.

9. Invite the rest of the participants to comment on whether the level of revenge is suitable for the scenario.

Exploration

- How was it waiting to see what number player two would roll?

- How much power did you have over the revenge they took?

- When was the situation in your control?

- Is that like real life?

- Are there unwritten rules about levels of revenge?

- What happens if they are broken?

- Does the ante get upped or stay on the same level?

- What happens if the level of revenge escalates?

- What would happen if you didn't take revenge?

- How else could you get your needs met?

- What are the alternatives to revenge that will keep you in high status/reputation?

Comments

There are unwritten rules relating to appropriate levels of revenge in gang conflict. For instance, if a gang member's car has been burnt out by a member of the rival gang, it may be considered appropriate to beat up a rival gang member. It may be inappropriate in this instance to beat up the mother of a rival gang member. The difficulty with revenge is that the stakes tend to get raised, often resulting in serious injury. The act of taking revenge results in a loss of power because once revenge has been taken the control is given away. Revenge is tied up with issues of status and reputation because not taking revenge can be considered a weakness. Groups can be encouraged to think about alternatives to revenge that will not result in giving up status and reputation. An example of this would be a mediation session between rival gangs where unresolved issues are aired and an attempt to find common ground is made.

The Gamble of Revenge scenario cards

1. Your younger brother has been kidnapped by a rival gang who are the same age as him (three years younger than you). They have beaten him up and dropped him back where they picked him up from.

2. Your phone was stolen from you on the street by a group of young men you have seen around.

3. A group of young people you have not seen before walks past you and one of them barges you.

4. Local young people have been throwing stones at your mum.

5. A group of ten 21-year-olds have recently started hanging around your area dealing cocaine.

6. Your best friend made a racist comment to a member of your rival gang. A week later your best friend was beaten up by this gang.

7. You're walking down the street alone and three young people pass you and laugh at your trainers.

Taking the Work Forward

There are many different ways in which gangs work can be taken forward. Throughout the programme relationships will develop between group members and between the participants and the adults who have been facilitating the programme.

During the programme the adults may notice individuals who would be suited to taking a facilitating role in future gangs programmes. These young people can be nurtured and developed with the possibility of a future career in Youth and Community work. Other participants may have identified alternative paths they would like to take and the adults may be able to offer practical support around these choices.

A typical outcome of a structured gangs programme is that the group will have strengthened their cohesiveness and have a heightened sense of their personal and group identity. This is a powerful place to be as the group has in many ways moved towards being a potential agent of social change. For example, ideas around the conditions that can create a context for gang conflict developing may have been discussed. The group may then want to use this learning to inform decision makers by making specific recommendations around future policy, e.g. work with town planners to explore the relationship between housing policy and territorialism.

Often gangs that are engaged in conflict will have shared concerns and similar material needs. This can be a useful starting point for joint work as common ground can be usefully established. The content of a joint meeting will depend on the context of the conflict between the two groups. As both groups will have experienced the same groupwork programme revisiting some of the exercises in this manual can be useful. The gangs will recognise they have had a common experience of the groupwork, have had an opportunity to hear each other's stories and also get a sense of how they have moved on from their first experience of the exercise.

When there is a long history of violent conflict it may be helpful for any joint meetings to take the form of mediation or a Restorative Justice conference. If the local workers are not trained in these techniques they might consider bringing in experienced mediators or facilitators of Restorative Justice conferences. Alternatively, where the conflict has been more random, e.g. the targeting of young people because they are from a different ethnic group, it might be more relevant for the groups to spend the joint meeting exploring and sharing their cultural identities. For instance, at the first joint meeting of a group of African Caribbean and Somali young people the groups created identity shields and found common ground in their history of immigration, experiences of racism and shared ancestral roots in Africa.

In situations where there is a long history of fighting between gangs there is the potential to train group members in mediation techniques so that when other gangs find themselves in similar positions there are trained mediators on hand to offer support. The mediation can be set up so the mediators are from different gangs, thus modelling how these groups can work together as well as having the benefit of the mediators having experienced and found their way through the conflict. The groups may decide they would like to develop a project of their own creation, e.g. a peer mentoring project, and the adult staff could support them with linking in with local schools and youth provision.

Our experience in developing and delivering this groupwork programme has been that it can be a powerful tool for engaging young people's hearts and minds in actively reflecting on the choices they make in their lives. Harnessing young people's voices, energy and enthusiasm can be one of the key factors in developing safer more cohesive communities, and beginning the process of developing the community leaders of the future. Young people from one of the first Gangs programmes we ran went on to take up positions as mentors, volunteers and paid workers in their local Youth Service – consequently playing an active role in supporting other young people. Several young people from a variety of our Gangs programmes have been invited to speak at conferences at which key decision makers have been present, thus informing future policy.

We hope that this manual provides you with some tools and techniques for beginning or strengthening the process of young people creating different choices and futures for themselves, which in turn has a favourable impact on your local communities.

Appendix

A description and summary of the learning from Leap's Gangs and Territorialism action research project

The following is a review of the findings from Leap's exploration into the experiences of young people involved in gang activity in the UK. Leap recognised the need to identify and understand the issues from the grassroots before exploring potential interventions. Action research was chosen as a methodology because this form of data collection allows the intervention itself to produce data which would not normally be gained from other research techniques. This data is then fed back into the intervention creating a dialectical relationship. Below are the findings of the focus groups and a description of how this information was used to inform pilot projects that took place in different parts of the country.

Focus groups

Over a period of 18 months we spoke to 330 young people from 30 youth organisations throughout the UK. The organisations were contacted in a variety of ways. Some were existing contacts, others were 'cold called' by the Gangs team as they were working in an area we were particularly interested in, and some got in touch with Leap as they had heard about the work. The average age of respondents was 15.4 years and 75 per cent of those spoken to were male, of whom 47 per cent were white, 33 per cent African/African Caribbean, 17 per cent Asian and 3 per cent other.

Each focus group lasted approximately 90 minutes. They generally took place in youth centres and were supported mainly by outreach workers who had developed relationships with the gangs. The focus groups used a variety of interactive methods to explore themes of gangs and territorialism. Since the subject matter was of relevance and interest to the groups there was very little problem keeping the young people on task. The focus groups started with introductions and a warm-up game exploring different types of conflict. Wordstorming exercises and discussion were then used to explore three key questions:

1. What is a gang?

2. Why are young people in gangs?

3. What is the difference between a gang and a group of friends?

The young people were then asked to fill in short questionnaires which asked a series of questions relating to local gang activity and their group of friends.

A combination of the flip-chart notes from the wordstorming exercises, the completed questionnaires and transcripts of the sessions provided the gangs workers with rich and varied sources of data. The main objective of the analysis was to explore the role of the gang so that the learning could be used to inform the pilot projects.

The greatest benefit of being in a gang was protection (30.6%) whilst the greatest disadvantage of being in a gang reported by gang members was violence (30%). The main reason young people gave for being in a gang was having nothing to do.

The research pointed towards a clear opportunity to harness the energy and companionship of the gang and turn it into new opportunities for leadership and learning. The analysis also highlighted the need for more in-depth examination of the characteristics, values and opinions of young people, particularly those who consider themselves gang members. Increasing recreational activities offers young people new experiences, but it is also important to provide a structured programme that addresses the key recurrent themes that emerged from the focus groups: safety, danger, space, territorialism, status, reputation, enemies and revenge. These themes were central to the groupwork devised by the Gangs team for the pilot projects.

Talking to people working with young people in gangs

The Gangs team recognised the value of learning from practitioners already engaged in working with young people in gangs. They spoke to over 100 agencies representing a wide spectrum of organisation type, throughout the UK, USA and Europe.

Very few practitioners in the UK are specifically responsible for working with young people in gangs although many are doing the work, mainly through outreach. Variations between the types of gang, and therefore the type of intervention, varied enormously from city to city and within cities. For example, the Gangs team spoke to an organisation in Belfast that chose to engage young people in single identity work, despite more funding being available for work taking place with both Protestant and Catholic young people. Their reasoning was that the young people they were working with were so disengaged and lacking in self-esteem that it was enough for them to get involved in self-exploration without also being confronted by their enemies. In contrast to this, work in a North London borough involved bringing together groups of young people who were engaged in conflict from three different local youth clubs. Each of these youth clubs was predominantly attended by young people from a particular ethnicity and the work focused on bringing together young people from different ethnic groups for a football tournament.

The research experience and findings in the USA varied enormously. The Gangs team was able to visit a multitude of organisations specifically working with gangs. These organisations varied from state-wide police programmes to ex-gang members doing outreach work from small organisations. Virtually every programme visited incorporated an anti-gang strategy with the aim being for young people to leave the gang. There is not the same emphasis on work with gangs in the UK because the costs of being in a gang are not so high. According to statistics compiled by the Violence Prevention Coalition of Greater Los Angeles, in Los Angeles county there were 349 gang-related deaths in 1999, which is not comparable with the UK experience. The Gangs team learnt that despite clear similarities in the reasons for young people joining gangs in the UK and USA, the levels of violence are very different.

Literature review

In order to develop a detailed understanding of the issues surrounding youth involvement in gang activity an extensive literature review was undertaken. The Gangs team quickly learned that there had been no major piece of research into the UK experience of gangs since the 1970s. The more recent literature is written about US gangs and therefore reflects the US experience.

For much of the twentieth century the Chicago School of sociological thought was the dominant paradigm for understanding gangs. This thinking was formulated between the world wars and focused on urban social relationships at a time of mass migration and immigration. It is characterised as viewing gang members as deviant and a product of the urban disorganisation of working-class communities. Thrasher (1927) saw gangs as integrated groups, bound together by conflict with the wider community, with a strong sense of loyalty and commitment to each other. Similarly, Cohen (1955) treated working-class gangs as subcultures that rejected middle-class values and argued that being in a gang provided a solution to the experience of status frustration.

UK literature developed from the research that had been taking place in the USA. Sociologists were beginning to move away from the view that gangs were tightly bound groups. Scott (1956) groups gangs into three categories: adolescent street groups; gangs proper; and loosely structured or diffuse groups. Cohen (1972) viewed gangs as 'loose collectivities or crowds within which there was occasionally some more structured grouping, based on territorial loyalty'. Patrick (1974) notes that 'the Glasgow juvenile gang has little internal cohesion of its own; it exists to oppose others'. He found that gangs were centred around old housing areas and were a 'long-standing Glasgow institution'.

More contemporary US thinking moves away from the view of the gang member as necessarily 'deviant'. Venkatesh (2003) notes that flouting social codes and laws is only part of the experience of a gang member. He also acknowledges the 'inequity that may exist among the communities as well as the numerous nondelinquent aspects of the activity (e.g. resource distribution, political resistance, articulation of a belief or ideal)'. When looking at gangs and their relationship to territory, Brotherton (2000) theorises that working-class youths do not 'hang out' in public spaces because they are lazy. Instead it is a 'forced outgrowth and reaction to industrial society's authority over time, space and age segregation'. Hence 'hanging out' can be seen as a way of showing outward resistance to the status quo.

Pilot project – Castlemilk

The first of the pilot projects took place in Castlemilk, a large housing scheme 5 km south of Glasgow. Castlemilk has a longstanding history of gang fighting and territorial disputes as well as an impressive history of youth interventions. A youth-led research project in 1998 concluded that territorial boundaries did exist, gang membership was linked to geography, gangs were associated with violence and many young people's lives were affected by the existence of gangs, both negatively and positively.

The pilot Gangs and Territorialism project involved a multi-agency team of local workers in a 12-week summer project. The local workers used their specialist knowledge and previously established relationships to identify and recruit young people to the programme. The local workers were given three days of conflict resolution training, which provided them with a grounding in understanding and responding to conflict and also served to develop a cohesive team. Nurturing and developing these relationships was key to the success of the project.

Three self-identified gangs of young people were engaged in a programme of intensive groupwork activities. The locally agreed aim of the project was for young people to be able to make informed choices on gang membership, through exploring their identity, sense of belonging and the costs and gains of being in a gang. Overall 57 young people took part in the programme. Their ages ranged between 11 and 18, with the vast majority being 14- to 16-year-olds. All the young people were white Scottish, with 37 males and 20 females.

Young people in Castlemilk were keen to explore gang membership and the conflicts that arose from being in a gang. They were not open to being told they should or should not be in a gang or to being told to stop gang fighting. In many ways gang fighting was considered to be a fairly harmless activity. However, the lack of access to certain areas and resources resulting from fear of attack was considered a greater problem. It was important to work with the infrastructure of the group itself, which included highlighting the roles that each young person plays and exploring the internal conflicts within the group. The groupwork also looked at the history of past conflicts between different groups and between the young people and the police and acknowledged any historical injustices.

The project culminated in a residential programme bringing together self-selected young people from three of the gangs. A residential trip was chosen as a method of working as it allows the groupwork to develop with a certain amount of intensity and continuity. It also acts as an incentive to the young people participating in the programme. Team spirit is achieved both inside and outside the training room and incidents that happen outside the training room can be dealt with inside the training room.

The result of this work has included separate reports from the young people, youth workers and schools workers, all of which highlight less violence and fighting in schools at the beginning of the autumn term. The issues between gangs did not build up over the summer period and hence were not then brought into school as would normally happen. Young people reported that being a part of the project left them with a sense of being valued and important. It gave them an opportunity to discuss their experiences as gang members and explore issues that affected their lives.

Key learning points

- Working with local practitioners who had already established relationships with the gang members was vital.

- Having a multi-agency team of local and Leap workers involved in the project planning workshops meant the project's aim was relevant to Castlemilk whilst incorporating the specialist skills of the Gangs team.

- Training for local practitioners in conflict resolution skills and gang awareness helped to share knowledge and build a cohesive team.

- The Leap workers coming from outside the area contributed to the work as they were considered neutral, interested and as having something new to offer by the young people.

- The project would have benefited if a short A5 information sheet had been drafted and an open meeting called for other practitioners, community members and parents.

- The activities were an attraction for getting young people involved, diverted them from the streets and offered structured recreation for the gang as a whole.

- Each gang has a different internal dynamic, thus being flexible with the group work ensured that the work was relevant and suitable for individual gangs.

- How gang members were chosen for the residential was integral to the gangs feeling safe and well represented.

- Gang leaders and influential members of the gang need to be considered carefully as the relationship held with them will affect the programme.

Pilot Project – King's Cross, London

Building on the learning from the first pilot project, the second pilot project took place in King's Cross, London. The project was a collaboration between Leap and the young people and workers from a variety of organisations in the London Borough of Camden, led by Camden Youth and Connexions Service.

Leap was approached by a collection of Camden youth workers because of Leap's specialist conflict resolution work in the areas of gangs and territorialism. The workers were based at two youth centres less than two miles apart, visited by two groups of predominantly Bangladeshi young men. There was a history of tension between these groups that had become more apparent in recent years as the number and ferocity of violent confrontations increased.

Following a series of planning meetings it was agreed that the pilot project would use conflict resolution techniques and theatre to promote understanding between the two groups. Using their local knowledge, a multi-agency team of workers identified and recruited the young people onto the programme. The project took place over a period of six months and culminated in a residential. Each week the two groups individually received 2.5 hours of focused groupwork. 20 young people aged between 16 and 18 took part in the programme.

The response of the young people to the work was extremely positive at the outset. They showed a willingness and interest in reflecting on their experiences of group conflict and trusted the workers with personal details about their lives. Initially both groups were keen to meet with a view to resolving the conflict once some groundwork had been done.

Two months into the work a violent confrontation took place involving some of the members of the groups. The conflict was part of an ongoing dispute between the leaders of the two groups. This resulted in a decision to continue working with the groups individually rather than doing the originally planned joint work. It was apparent that for some young people their identity and status were so deeply rooted in their position in the gang that resolving the conflict between the groups would leave them feeling undermined.

The work has benefited the young people in many different ways. Of those involved in the project 60 per cent have moved into paid or voluntary work as a direct consequence of their involvement in the project. One of the groups has presented at a conference and edited a video of their experiences, which will be used as a peer education tool. Funding has been achieved to continue working with the groups at a local level and there is still hope from workers and some young people that dialogue might take place between the rival gangs.

Key learning points

- Whilst having local workers with existing relationships with the young people is vital, care and thought must be given to the nature of these relationships. For example, one of the groups held one of the youth workers in such high esteem that they were reluctant to divulge anything that showed themselves in a negative light.

- Having youth workers representing the two different areas in conflict was vital to the success of the project.

- Agreement needs to be received early on for the participants' names to be shared with each group.

- The group leader's status will change when joint work takes place and this needs to be managed carefully.

- Bringing two antagonistic groups together arouses anxieties amongst group members and should be used very carefully as a means of responding to their conflict. Bridges can be built between groups without them having to meet.

- It is important to respond to conflict that happens outside the project by focusing on the conflict and its impact upon their lives and people around them. The work should be based in and explore the realities of the conflict.

References

Baime, C., Brookes, S., and Mountford, A. (2002) *Geese Theatre Handbook*. Winchester: Waterside Press.

Boal, A. (1992) *Games for Actors and Non-Actors*. London: Routledge.

Brotherton, D.C. (2000) *Old Heads Tell Their Stories: From Street Gangs to Street Organizations: A Comparative Analysis of Youth Street Subcultures in New York City*. New York: Sociology Department, John Jay College of Criminal Justice. City University of New York.

Cohen, A.K. (1955) *Delinquent Boys: The Culture of the Gang*. New York: Free Press.

Cohen, S. (1972) *Folk Devils and Moral Panics*. London: Paladin.

Fine, N. (1996) *Through the Walls*. Belleville, South Africa: Community Law.

Fine, N. and Macbeth, F. (1995) *Playing With Fire: Creative Conflict Resolution for Young Adults*. Columbia: New Society.

Jung, C.G. (1981) The Archetypes and The Collective Unconscious (Collected Works of C.G. Jung Vol. 9 Part 1). Princeton, NJ: Bollingen.

Patrick, J. (1974) *A Glasgow Gang Observed*. London: Eyre Methuen.

Scott, P.D. (1956) 'Gangs and delinquent groups in London.' *British Journal of Delinquency, 1*, 4–24.

Thrasher, F.M. (1927) *The Gang: A Study of 1,313 Gangs in Chicago*. Chicago, IL: Chicago University Press.

Venkantesh, S. (2003) 'A note on social theory and the American street gang.' In L. Kontos, D. Brotherton and L. Barrios (eds) *Gangs and Society: Alternative Perspectives*. New York: Columbia University Press.

About Leap

The work of the Gangs and Territorialism project builds on existing work that Leap Confronting Conflict has done since 1987 in partnership with Youth, Education and Criminal Justice services. Leap is the only youth organisation with the explicit vision that the living processes of conflict resolution and mediation should lie at the heart of personal and social education for all young people.

By training young people in self-awareness, personal accountability, listening to others, communication and mediation skills, we engage young people's intellect, heart and spirit. By training adults we build their confidence and skills and renew their enthusiasm and motivation for their work.

Leap offers a variety of training courses for young people and adults who work with young people in a professional capacity. Leap also offers training and consultancy for individuals and their organisations. Leap's Gangs and Territorialism Project continues to work in partnership with agencies nationwide, delivering structured groupwork programmes to young people and to adults working with young people in gangs.

> Leap Confronting Conflict…provides very good quality training for young people and adult practitioners… Leap provides an imaginative range of programmes based on creative use of conflict for personal development. (Ofsted Extended Monitoring Report, July 2004)

For more information about Leap Confronting Conflict please call +44 (207) 272 5630, email us at info@leaplinx.com, or visit our website www.leaplinx.com.